HOW HAVE
Great
Small Group
Meetings

Dozens of Ideas You Can Use Right Now

DR. NEAL F. McBRIDE

NavPress
BRINGING TRUTH TO LIFE
NavPress Publishing Group
P.O. Box 35001, Colorado Springs, Colorado 80935

The Navigators is an international Christian organization. Our mission is to reach, disciple, and equip people to know Christ and to make Him known through successive generations. We envision multitudes of diverse people in the United States and every other nation who have a passionate love for Christ, live a lifestyle of sharing Christ's love, and multiply spiritual laborers among those without Christ.

NavPress is the publishing ministry of The Navigators. Nav-Press publications help believers learn biblical truth and apply what they learn to their lives and ministries. Our mission is to stimulate spiritual formation among our readers.

Library of Congress Catalog Card Number:
       97-9828
ISBN 1-57683-021-7

Some of the anecdotal illustrations in this book are true to life and are included with the permission of the persons involved. All other illustrations are composites of real situations, and any resemblance to people living or dead is coincidental.

Unless otherwise identified, all Scripture quotations in this publication are taken from the *Holy Bible:New International Version* (NIV). Copyright © 1973, 1978, 1984 by International Bible Society. Used by permission of Zondervan Publishing House. All rights reserved. Another version used is the *New American Standard Bible* (NASB), © The Lockman Foundation 1960, 1962, 1963, 1968, 1971, 1972, 1973, 1975, 1977.

McBride, Neal
       How to have great small group meetings : dozens of
       ideas you can use right now / Neal F. McBride.
              p.   cm.
       ISBN 1-57683-021-7 (paper)
       1. Church group work. 2. Small groups. I. Title.
BV652.2.M365   1997
253'.7—dc21   97-9828
                                                       CIP
Printed in the United States of America

2 3 4 5 6 7 8 9 10 11 12 13 14 15 / 99

Contents

Dedicated to the Grace University
Students, Faculty, and Staff
Omaha, Nebraska

Thank you for allowing me to serve
with and among you.

Introduction

Welcome! Since you're reading this book, you're probably a group leader or a potential group leader who wants to conduct great group meetings. With that in mind, here's my first tip: *Great small groups rarely just happen.* Most often it takes careful planning and skilled leadership. Don't get me wrong. It's possible to have great meetings without planning and good leadership, just don't bank on it happening. Conversely, proficient leadership and diligent planning offer no guarantees. The odds, however, are stacked in your favor *if* you invest time, energy, and, most importantly, prayer in planning your group meetings.

I want to develop one basic, key point in this book: *Great small group meetings happen by design, not default.* Know what you're going to do and do it well! There is no legitimate substitute for careful planning guided by the Holy Spirit.

Great meetings demand that you develop skills in two important dimensions: relationships and processes. Furthermore, excellent meetings require careful planning of what happens before and after meetings, as well as of the actual meetings themselves. We'll consider all these issues.

PROCEED WITH CAUTION! Group leadership skills, methods, and even meticulous planning cannot replace the need for being God's servant. Your relationship with Jesus Christ and dependence on the Holy Spirit must have first priority. Good group leadership and great meetings are based more on successful relationships with God and between the group members than on methods. Methods are important tools—become as skilled as possible—but you cannot ignore the spiritual dimension if you want truly great meetings.

In this book I share with you the experiences and insights God has given me in the nearly three decades I've been involved with small groups. They're my experiences; they're not the law. Feel free to disagree with me, and do it your way. What works for me may not be appropriate in your situation. Nevertheless, my desire is to help you avoid as much as possible the "trial-by-error" path most leaders experience on their journey to becoming good small group leaders and having great meetings.

Accept a simple fact: Becoming an excellent small group leader takes time. Be patient with yourself. It doesn't happen overnight. Remember the old saying, "Rome was not built in a day" (an obvious but beneficial notion)? The time you invest is well spent.

One side thought. Perhaps you're like me—you make a better coach than a player. Great teams need great coaches. Maybe your future role is to train, motivate, and encourage *other* group leaders rather than leading a group yourself. If this is the case, you'll need the guidance provided in this book to build your own skills first and then to help others do likewise.

Lord willing, this book will help you plan and conduct great meetings—meetings your entire group enjoys and benefits from. Two earlier books lay the foundation for what I share in this volume:

How to Lead Small Groups
Neal F. McBride, NavPress, 1990

How to Build a Small Groups Ministry
Neal F. McBride, NavPress, 1995

If you haven't read these books, especially *How to Lead Small Groups*, you may find it helpful to do so prior to reading this book. Much of what I want to share with you is rooted in the principles discussed in my previous books. Nevertheless, this book can stand on its own and will cover the following topics:

Chapter one is essentially an overview, a quick look at some foundational materials to set the stage for planning and conducting great small group meetings. You'll see why a small group leader must first have a right relationship with God, and you'll review such issues as motivation, group purpose and goals, leadership, and covenanting as a group.

Chapter two lays out a strategy to plan great meetings. Effective planning is an underlying requirement for having successful meetings. This chapter helps you develop a planning structure, write your objectives, select activities and methods, and put together the meeting's details.

Chapter three focuses on helping the people in your group become effective group members. Great meetings are meetings where everyone feels comfortable participating at a level they choose. This chapter considers such issues as members' expectations, participation, and involvement.

Chapter four develops the idea—"Variety is the spice of life." You and your group's VQ (variety quotient) is explored. This chapter helps you understand variety, how it's applied, and some things to avoid, while presenting ten variety guidelines.

Chapter five deals with group spontaneity. You'll discover what the Bible has to say about spontaneity, the Holy Spirit's role, how to apply spontaneity, and when not to deviate from your meeting plan.

Chapter six examines the leader's responsibility to serve as a model. Beginning with a look at the apostle Paul's example, this chapter considers the group leader's role as a model in setting the group's atmosphere and pace, and it concludes with a brief discussion on shared leadership.

Chapter seven puts it all together and talks about actually conducting great meetings. This chapter examines functional issues such as a premeeting checklist, getting started and finishing on time, staying on track, helping members participate, flexing to meet needs, and knowing when to quit.

Chapter eight wraps up the book by presenting some helpful ideas and suggestions for great meetings. Workable options include group service projects, playing together, meeting with other groups, special occasions, prayer partners and chains, outreach, and the group saying, "I'm sorry."

Concluding each chapter is a **Taking Action** section designed to help you apply the material you just read in that particular chapter. The assignments are helpful and brief.

Thanks for joining me in our mutual quest for great small group meetings! May God grant you insight and wisdom as you read this book.

CHAPTER ONE

Foundations:
The Necessary
Prerequisites

Of course, you want to have great group meetings and, ultimately, a successful group. Do you know any group leaders who intentionally set out to have poor, ineffective group meetings? I don't. No one wants to fail. You accepted a small group ministry, or are considering such a ministry, because you envisioned success. Praise God! Success is possible!

To a large degree, success as a group leader means planning and conducting great group meetings. But such meetings don't just happen; they actually begin before the group has its first meeting and then continue after the group's meetings conclude.

Certain basic elements or foundations are necessary to set the stage for producing effective group meetings. Making certain these required foundations are securely in place vastly increases the potential for initial and ongoing success. Conversely, if the foundations aren't set in concrete, your chances at building a really great group aren't good.

Basic ingredients are needed. Just as you cannot bake a cake without flour, certain basic ingredients are necessary to develop and have great group meetings. Consequently, this first chapter attempts to review some essential, foundational ideas upon which great meetings depend. If we were building a house, this chapter would be the foundation. The remaining chapters assist you in building the "walls" and "roof." Even if you're familiar with the basic building blocks, I encourage you to take the time to review this chapter. So let's get started.

BEING RIGHT WITH GOD FIRST

Great group meetings require more than a bag of tricks. Even though this book focuses on helping you increase your small group leadership techniques, great group meetings cannot be viewed as merely using the right methods and doing the right things. Your first priority is a secure, growing relationship with Jesus Christ. Correct knowledge and skills come *after* establishing a right walk with God. Who we are in Christ is more important than what we do for God, even though we understand "that faith without deeds is useless" (James 2:20). Both faith *and* works are essential, but it's a matter of priorities. Our priorities must be in order—faith in God first, then appropriate works.

Your best preparation for leading a small group is to nurture your walk with God and remain open to His leading in your life. Small group ministry, or any ministry for that matter, is only as effective as your intimacy with Jesus Christ and sensitivity to the Holy Spirit's leading. Christ comes first! (Matthew 6:33). Yet there is another element in your relationship with God you must deal with before we can discuss the other foundations for great group meetings.

GETTING MOTIVATED

Whose glory are you seeking to promote? What are your motives? Your answers to these probing questions reflect your true motivation for wanting to lead a successful group. Ideally your first desire should be to please God and bring glory and honor to Him (Colossians 3:17). However, be honest with yourself. Perhaps deep down you're also interested in receiving a little credit for doing a good job? Yes? I hope so. *It's natural for you to want to do a good job and share in the credit.* Nevertheless, note I said, "Share in the credit." If your principal reason for leading a group is to receive all the attention and credit for yourself, then you're off base. Christ must receive credit and honor first. Then, if you benefit from His being honored, receive it with humility (Luke 14:11).

Motivation is a tricky thing to deal with. I've never encountered a small group leader who admitted wanting to lead a group for self-serving, ulterior reasons. "Good" Christians just don't do such a thing. Yet several people I've dealt with wanted to lead small groups for what in my opinion seemed like questionable reasons—not stated reasons. Oh, no!

Yet they demonstrated attitudes and behavior that revealed dubious motives. One person was a former pastor who wanted "his" group to "really study God's Word." Sounds good, but what he actually exhibited was a need to control people and have a platform to preach, which he called "sharing" because it took place in a small group.

Think about it. What's *your* real motive for leading a small group? Lord willing, you're able to say your primary motive is to glorify God, and then, if success happens, you can have the satisfaction of having done a good job. It's okay to personally benefit from doing a good job, *if your primary goal was/is to magnify Jesus Christ* and not yourself (Hebrews 5:4).

To summarize up to this point, the critical cornerstones for a really great group are your relationship with Christ and your motivation for leadership. These spiritual foundations are not optional, but essential. Proceeding on without first insuring these bricks are in place is unadvised. However, once they are in place, you're ready to proceed. But remember: Your relationship with Christ and motivation for leadership are elements you must continue to nurture. They require your never-ending attention. Now let's turn to some functional foundations necessary to have great small group meetings.

STATING A PURPOSE AND SETTING GOALS

I don't know if it's original with her, but Dr. Roberta Hestenes, former president of Eastern College in Pennsylvania and now a pastor in California, offered an excellent observation during her speech at a small groups conference I attended in California some time ago. When it came to questions about small groups, she suggested a brilliant answer, one I wish I had thought of but, nevertheless, use all the time. She wisely advised the universal answer to most small group questions, which is *"It all depends."* Right on! Answers to most questions link back to and depend on the group's purpose and goals.

Why does your group exist? What is its purpose? What do you hope to accomplish? These basic questions are what I immediately pose when leaders ask me questions about their groups. Without this information, it's difficult to determine a right course of action or to offer useful advice. Your group's purpose and goals set the framework and define the group's existence.

Too frequently groups attempt to function without knowing why they exist or what they hope to achieve. Time and energy is invested, but it's often wasted effort because it lacks direction. Therefore, it's wise for us to briefly define "purpose" and "goals."

Purpose = Why the group exists; the type of group or main reason for the group to meet; the group's focus.

Goals = Related to your purpose, what you specifically want to accomplish; "measurable" results you are seeking to achieve by being a group.

What Is the Purpose?

A group's purpose gives the group intentionality and direction. Stating a purpose creates a reason, mission, or rationale for the group's existence. When answering the question, Why does the group exist or meet? you are taking an important first step in the journey toward conducting great group meetings. After all, how can you plan and conduct excellent meetings if you don't have any idea why the group meets? It seems obvious, but I'm amazed at how many groups lack a clear purpose for existing.

A clearly defined purpose is usually reflected in the type of group you have or want. Groups provide a useful ministry format or method to accomplish many things. As such, a group must have a purpose for existing—that is, a primary reason for functioning. Although the group's activities may differ from meeting to meeting, the central purpose remains fixed.

What kinds of groups are possible? If you've read extensively about small groups, you already know numerous lists are available. Each author suggests his or her own listing. For myself, I suggest four basic or generic group types. These four types lend themselves to many different applications and adaptations.

I won't take much time to review the four types of groups I recommend because the topic is dealt with in my previous NavPress books, *How to Lead Small Groups* and *How to Build a Small Groups Ministry.* Nevertheless, here is a quick overview:

Relationship (or process) groups—The focus is on group processes to establish and nurture interpersonal relationships among the members as brothers and sisters in Christ. As God's children, they need to encourage and build up one another (1 Thessalonians 5:11). Groups in this category are often called "growth groups," "caring groups," "fellowship groups," "covenant groups," or something similar. What the group does—its meeting format—is secondary to the primary focus on spiritual and/or social relationships.

Content groups—The primary purpose for these groups is to learn and discuss information—usually the Word of God, but not always. Relationship is important but secondary to covering and understanding the material. Little or no time is invested in group dynamics because the spotlight is on the content. Relationships and group process are often just assumed. Many Bible studies and discussion groups fit into this category.

Task groups—The central focus is on doing something (a job or responsibility) together as a group, usually some ministry. The group's defined task creates the purpose for meeting. Relationships among the group members usually take a secondary emphasis and might never be discussed until a problem arises. Task groups include most committees or planning groups, and even evangelism groups.

Need-based groups—The basic purpose is to provide support for fellow group members who have or are experiencing the same or similar need. Frequently called support or recovery groups, this type of group seeks to comfort one another (2 Corinthians 1:4). The options for need-oriented groups are endless. Recovery groups, support groups, self-help groups, and group counseling are all good examples.

My group types aren't a rigid, inspired classification system. Yet over the years, nearly every group I've ever run across easily fits into one of the four categories. I only suggest the four types so you can better think about and identify your group's purpose and goals. If my classifications work for you, great! If not, you're free to come up with your own system.

No single group type is preferred or ideal. All serve a purpose and can be useful. Which group type to choose boils down to what you want to accomplish. Moreover, for each type you can generate many different applications suitable to your situation. One caution: Attempting to achieve all the ideals reflected in the four types within one group is setting yourself up for a frustrating experience. If you want a "combination" group, I recommend not attempting to combine more than two basic types.

What Are the Goals?

Goals, objectives, aims, or whatever you wish to call them are linked to purpose. How many times have you heard the phrase: "If you aim at nothing, you'll surely hit it"? Well, you just read it again and it's still true. After determining why your group meets (its purpose), it's time to identify your group's goals. There is no escaping the fact that unless you have a fairly good idea of what you want to accomplish and some way to determine if and when you do, your group is likely to wander about and ultimately dissolve in disillusionment. I know because it's happened to me.

Clearly stating your group's purpose and goals is an important step toward becoming a successful group. I recommend you write down both your purpose and goals. There is something about putting it in writing that adds legitimacy to the process. The best tool for doing this is a covenant, a topic we'll consider later in this chapter.

Let me suggest one final idea related to purpose and goals before we move on and discuss leadership in the next section. "Vision" represents the ideal, desired situation or conditions I want to exist. It's a projected ideal future. Vision describes what you want to exist sometime in the future. Ideally, your group's purpose and goals reflect a clear vision.

Some individuals debate the verse's interpretation, but in my opinion, Proverbs 29:18 sets forth the vision standard: "Where there is no vision, the people are unrestrained" (NASB). The English word "unrestrained" in Hebrew is a primary root word that literally means "let go" or "let alone." In contemporary language, the idea or picture is of a people without a vision and everyone doing his or her own thing—diverse actions without direction or unity in purpose. To avoid the potential confusion that may result from everyone doing as he or she pleases, vision is a tool that provides focus, direction, cooperative action, and unity.

Your group's purpose and goals reflect the vision you have for your group. It's difficult to depend on the Holy Spirit for the wisdom and strength to accomplish what He desires unless you are able to "see" the group's future success. God gives you the vision. Subsequently your vision becomes a major criteria in determining the group's purpose and goals.

One last word about vision. Make certain it's a *shared* vision. As the leader or potential leader, it is easy to focus on explaining the meeting's details to your potential group members and not on helping them catch the vision for being a group. In fact, the best alternative is to enlist their involvement in developing the vision.

Long ago I learned to sell the vision for small groups and not focus on the mechanics associated with group formation and meetings. These latter details are important, but most potential group members are more interested in knowing the *why* than the *how*. In most cases the *how* becomes an issue only after they are excited about the *why*. Over the long haul, the *why* keeps the group motivated even when the *how* must be adjusted or completely changed.

STRIVING TO BE A GOOD LEADER

Great group meetings demand good leadership. In fact, my experience has taught me that leadership is the *key* to good groups. Under most circumstances, the equation is straightforward: Good leadership produces good groups. Conversely, poor leadership usually results in poor groups. It sounds too simple, but it's true. Don't overlook or dismiss this vital principle. Your role as a leader is critical to the group's success.

What is "good" leadership? Here are the seven characteristics that commonly distinguish an effective small group leader:

1. *Is a seasoned Christian* (1 Timothy 3:6). A good leader is mature in the faith and knows how to assist others in their faith development. I'm not suggesting any minimum or maximum time because it's different for every individual. Like human development, we all develop spiritually at different rates.
2. *Possesses a clearly demonstrated, growing personal relationship with Jesus Christ* (2 Peter 3:18). An effective group leader leads by lifestyle as much as with words and methods. Consequently, a leader must openly exhibit his or her relationship with Christ.
3. *Cares about people* (1 Corinthians 12:25). Leaders must be "people persons" by nature or willing to work at becoming such persons. Group ministry is people first, while systems, methods, and programs must take a secondary role.
4. *Enjoys serving people* (Galatians 5:13). A good group leader cares about people and is eager to translate that care into active service. Servant-leadership, exemplified by Jesus' earthly ministry, is the highest form of leadership in the body of Christ.

5. *Is willing to learn* (Ephesians 5:10). The best leaders are the ones who know what they don't know, understand what skills they need to develop, and are willing to take the necessary steps to acquire the needed knowledge and skills. Regardless of how much experience they have, wise leaders view themselves as ongoing learners.

6. *Articulates a vision for the small group* (Proverbs 29:18). Enthusiasm and the ability to "sell" members and potential members on the vision for the group is a key trait leaders should possess. The leader must have a vision for the group in order to set the pace for the group.

7. *Wants to spend the necessary time* (Ecclesiasties 3:1, NASB). When it comes down to it, the good leader is willing to invest the time it takes to lead the group effectively. Ministry takes time.

Whoa! Your immediate reaction after reading the previous list is "I'm not qualified to lead a group." Don't be so hard on yourself. You can do it! Claim and practice the apostle Paul's perspective: "I can do all things through [Christ] who strengthens me" (Philippians 4:13, NASB). The list represents an ideal to obtain, not the absolute minimum to serve. If you're like me and most other small group leaders, you haven't nailed down every qualification. Just make sure you're committed to working on the areas (with God's help) that aren't your strengths.

Note that the list doesn't include anything about knowledge of or experience with small groups. These are desirable qualifications, but not necessary. The good leader, or someone with the potential to become a good leader, demonstrates a commitment to the ministry and a willingness to learn the necessary information and skills. I can work with someone who is inexperienced and willing to learn, but not with someone who has tremendous knowledge and skill but isn't willing to serve or who isn't a team player.

Becoming an effective leader takes time. Be patient with yourself. Yet there is more to it than merely allowing time to pass. You must invest the time wisely while increasing your knowledge and skills. Becoming a good leader and conducting great meetings requires time, experience, information, and mastering certain tasks. Your expertise will grow, Lord willing, *if* you become a student of small groups and use your time prudently.

ESTABLISHING A GROUP COVENANT

There is no doubt in my mind that a covenant is among the most important tools you can use to help insure your group's success. It's an *essential* foundation. In fact, I'm so convinced a covenant is necessary that I'm bold enough to suggest groups who don't use one, or something similar, are more likely to fail than to succeed. As you can tell, I'm sold on drafting and using a group covenant.

Some individuals call them a "group contract," but I prefer the biblical term "covenant." God is our model for using covenants. Scripture presents the "Old" and "New" Covenants, which govern the relationship between God and man, and man and his fellow man. Based on the biblical model, a small group covenant is a written compact or agreement that sets forth specific details, principles, and practices the group members commit themselves to uphold for the specified period of time they meet together as a group.

A covenant is essential because it is a tool to help:

◆ Establish the group's purpose and goals
◆ Clarify the expectations members have for being in the group
◆ Set membership norms (boundaries or standards)
◆ Promote "team building" and the group's formation
◆ Provide a standard for evaluating the group's progress
◆ Facilitate any changes that may arise
◆ Communicate the group's expectations to potential new members

Drafting a Covenant

Having a covenant is more important than its exact form or format. Several different types are discussed in my book *How to Build a Small Group Ministry.*

Ideally, you should include all your group members in drafting the covenant. Set several weeks aside early in the group's existence, or perhaps even before the group begins to meet, to discuss your covenant and to draft its specific elements. Covenants can be long and detailed or short and general. My usual strategy is to prepare a one-page suggested covenant and encourage the members to edit the document—adding, subtracting, or altering elements. This "priming-the-pump" method avoids spinning your wheels and gets things going. I've seen it take three or four meetings before everyone in the group is comfortable with the proposed covenant and before it's finally adopted. Even if it takes longer, it's worth the time invested.

Using a Covenant

Merely having a covenant isn't the object; it requires use. Once a covenant is drafted and adopted, the successful group then uses the document to guide the group's further development and evaluate its progress. In *How to Lead Small Groups*, I refer to this process as involving both "formative" and "summative" evaluation. Formative evaluation seeks to help the group make whatever adjustments are necessary to accomplish its purpose and goals while the group is still meeting as a group. View it as in-flight adjustments. Summative evaluation takes place during the group's final weeks to determine how the group did overall. The aim is to determine if the purpose and goals were accomplished, to make decisions about going on as a group, and to know what to do or not do next time.

Using a covenant for evaluation needn't become a difficult or frightening experience. On a periodic basis (for example, every several months), set aside a few minutes at the beginning of a meeting to discuss how the group is doing (formative evaluation). Early in the group's life you may want to deal only with administrative details like meeting time, location, and format—nonpersonal issues. As the group members grow more comfortable with each other, and after the group has become or is close to becoming a true group and not just a collection of individuals, you may find it helpful to discuss your group dynamics, such as relationships, expectations, communications, and decision making. One important suggestion: STAY POSITIVE, even if your group is experiencing difficulties. If you allow the discussion to focus only on gripes, problems, or personal attacks, nothing is accomplished other than to further upset the members.

If you are using a covenant, and I hope you are (or are planning to do so), feel free to include the covenant itself as a document in your formative and summative evaluation. If the document needs to change to reflect your group's changing needs, so be it. *A covenant is merely a tool*, not inspired canon set in concrete.

PLANNING MEETINGS EFFECTIVELY

One last critical foundation for having great small group meetings: In the vast majority of cases, great meetings demand and reflect adequate planning. "Winging" your group meetings rarely works more than once or twice. There is simply no getting around it; ample and sufficient planning is required (Proverbs 21:5).

A well-planned meeting involves many considerations that fit into two categories: (1) planning elements dealing with the group's purpose, goals, and design; and (2) planning the individual, specific group meetings. (My two previous books deal with category one at greater length than what is possible here. Meanwhile, the ideas, tips, and suggestions presented in this book mainly pertain to category two.)

With regard to category one, although I've already commented briefly on group purpose and goals at the beginning of this chapter, let me add several thoughts on planning the group's overall design. I use the term "design" to refer to definite issues related to nailing down organizational specifics (see step seven in *How to Build a Small Groups Ministry*) that are in keeping with the previously determined purpose and goals. Such matters as group size, when and how often you meet, where you meet, the general format and agenda, and the possible need for child care are issues related to how the group is generally structured and operates. Once these organizational elements are decided, you must plan the specific meetings themselves.

We are then ready to turn our attention to the second planning category. But remember, if the foundational considerations quickly reviewed in this first chapter (vision, purpose, goals, leadership, a group covenant, and group design) aren't in place, real success in planning great meetings is difficult to achieve.

Wait a second! Before you turn to chapter two, please take a few minutes to complete the final section in this chapter—"Taking Action." It's an opportunity to translate your knowledge into action. You'll have a similar opportunity at the end of each remaining chapter.

TAKING ACTION

1. As a prerequisite to leading great group meetings, your relationship with Jesus Christ should be secure and growing. Is it?

   _____ Yes.

   _____ No. (Okay, so what do you plan to do about it?)

2. Looking deep inside yourself, describe your motivations for being a small group leader. Do your motivations reflect correct attitudes and desires? Why or why not?

3. List your group's purpose and goals:

4. Which of the seven leadership characteristics do you see as your strengths, and which need further development?

5. What items are included in your group covenant?

6. Rate how important you think planning is to having great meetings (circle a number):

Not Important   Somewhat Important   Important   Very Important

1   2   3   4   5   6   7   8   9   10

7. How easy is planning for you? What obstacles do you encounter when you plan? How do you overcome them?

CHAPTER TWO

The Planning Process: Knowing Where You're Going

A failure to plan is a plan to fail. Yes, it's true! More group meetings fail due to deficient planning than to any other single cause. Conversely, diligent planning (see Proverbs 21:5) *potentially* yields successful group meetings. I say potentially because it's never a sure thing when dealing with unpredictable people (examined in chapter three), the dynamics associated with implementing the plan (discussed in chapter seven), and the potential for the Holy Spirit to override your plan (see chapter five). All things being equal, however, careful planning is the first step to successful groups.

I have a favorite saying: "Attention to small detail makes for a large success." In other words, success comes by paying attention to the many details necessary to accomplish a particular task. In our case, it's planning great small group meetings. And because planning is so important, even critical, this chapter is a little longer than the others.

Planning your small group meetings is much like preparing a Sunday school lesson. The context and dynamics are a bit different, but the two activities share common elements. So if you've ever taught a Sunday school class, you're already familiar with some of the ideas associated with planning small group meetings. You're not starting from ground zero, and most likely you're better prepared to plan your small group meetings than you anticipated.

As you would suspect, there is more than one way to plan small group meetings. Various strategies are possible. However, over the years I've developed a procedural pattern that seems to work consistently for

23

me: (1) prayer, (2) content, (3) objectives, (4) activities and methods, (5) details, and (6) follow-up. This six-step planning process works best with relationship-oriented groups and groups focusing on content. Using the proposed planning model to plan task and need-based group meetings usually requires some minor adjustments. I'll point out several as we go along.

Let me offer three pointers before we examine the six-step planning model for small group meetings. First, feel free to tailor the planning model to fit your situation. It isn't a rigid pattern requiring strict compliance. It's merely a suggested tool, and if something doesn't work for you, find a method that does. Second, the type of group (see chapter one) you are planning affects how you plan. You'll find each kind of group has its own unique planning needs. And third, the six planning steps may not always proceed in the exact order I describe. You may decide it's preferable to switch things around or even delete a step in some cases. In short, devise a planning strategy you feel comfortable with and one that fits your style.

Now let's examine each step in the six-step planning model.

EMPOWERING PLANNING THROUGH PRAYER

The role of prayer in planning is extremely critical. Your planning process must begin with, continue in, and conclude with prayer. In fact, when it comes to planning and conducting small group meetings, and every other aspect associated with small groups, Paul's admonition is right on: "Pray without ceasing" (1 Thessalonians 5:17, NASB).

Prayer is an indispensable planning tool because it connects you with God's power available only through the Holy Spirit. Without it, planning becomes little more than an administrative task accomplished with your human abilities. But saturated in prayer, planning is transformed into a supernatural endeavor. Wow! That's an exciting but sobering thought. We'll pick this topic up again in chapter five when we discuss following the Holy Spirit's lead in conducting your group meetings.

FOCUSING ON THE MEETING'S CONTENT

Content refers to the topic, substance, or anything else that serves as the focus around which your group meeting revolves. It's the information you want to cover, the skill you want to teach, or the attitude you seek to foster. For example, if the group is a Bible study (a content-oriented group), naturally the content is a specific verse, verses, chapter, or biblical theme. If yours is a task-oriented group, then the content is planning the task or actually doing some or all of the task. The content in relationship-oriented groups may include group-building skills, interpersonal communication, or even a Bible study that serves as the context for building relationships. Thus content can describe many possibilities and isn't limited to any one thing.

Usually your content is straightforward and easy to identify, but not always. On the one hand, if you're using a study guide or book, then each week you cover a selected chapter or portion (content) in sequence until you complete the entire book. In such cases it's fairly simple to identify your content. On the other hand, some need-oriented groups don't always have set content for each meeting. Their content is the dynamic associated with responding to the needs expressed by the group participants. Even so, well-planned meetings require you to identify your content, whatever that content may be.

Here are some suggested content options often associated with each kind of group (note: some content is suitable for more than one type of group):

Content Groups: Bible passage, chapter in a book, pastor's sermon, discussion topic, magazine article, poetry, academic subject, prayer, memorization, and so on.

Relationship Groups: Prayer, Bible study, discussion, social events, sharing significant life events, worship, sermon application, shared task, videos, singing, and so on.

Task Groups: Committee, governing board, choir, missions, youth ministry, drama, visitation, evangelism, prayer, worship, ushers, and so on.

Need-Based Groups: Recovery strategy, success stories, worship, personal sharing, prayer, encouragement, videos, coping skills, self-analysis, Bible study, and so on.

Group meetings may include more than one content area. Why? Some groups follow a set **format**, a fixed pattern that structures multiple activities during its weekly meetings. Each element in the format is included in the group's weekly agenda. Each requires a distinct activity that has its own purpose and corresponding content. Case in point, in discussing his "metachurch" model, Carl F. George suggests every group should include four essential actions: love (pastoral care), learn (Bible knowledge), decide (internal group administration), and do (duties that serve those outside the group). These key components serve as a structural framework—a format (my word)—for what he calls "cells" or groups. Cells are encouraged to include each element in their meetings even though the level, mix, or time for each may vary from one cell to the next; nevertheless, a meeting's agenda is structured around the four essential ingredients. Consequently, this implies there is different content for each segment, which obviously requires identification and planning.[1]

Once you determine the content of your small group meeting, spend whatever time is necessary to familiarize yourself with the material (facts, information, process, activity, event, and so on). How this is done depends on you. Use whatever study or preparation techniques that work for you. If you need assistance in this area, it's a good idea to talk with your pastor, buy a book at your local Christian bookstore or Christian college, borrow a book from a friend or your church library, or work with an experienced group leader. Do whatever you're comfortable with. It's your call.

Implementing an Agenda

Incidentally, one more planning concept that affects not only content but also every other element in our planning model needs to be briefly explored. I'm referring to using an **agenda**—an itinerary and schedule to guide the meeting.

Whether or not you use a fixed format, using an agenda to order your group meetings is a good idea. It's another important planning tool in your tool chest. A thought-out agenda helps you structure your format, content, objectives, activities, methods, and meeting details. It's a valuable device to organize your meeting. Specifically, your agenda sequences the meeting's exact *what, when,* and ideally *who.*

If you use a fixed format—that is, do the same thing every week—your agenda may or may not be fixed. Potential variations in the agenda may include the amount of time spent on each format element, the order in which things are done, or who does what. My advice is to experiment with your agenda. Keep the group meetings fresh and exciting even if the group's format is predictable from week to week. A good agenda structures your time in a realistic, efficient manner. The ideal agenda doesn't include too many activities, avoids allocating too much time or too little time for any one activity, uses the allotted time wisely, and accomplishes everything within the budgeted total time. Of course, these decisions are yours to make, and your skill in doing so comes with experience. Be patient with yourself. You're bound to make some mistakes.

Looking at a Sample Agenda

An agenda example is useful at this point. Let's say we are dealing with a relationship-oriented group that doesn't use a fixed format and we have ninety minutes to work with during each Tuesday evening. A workable agenda may look as follows (assuming everyone arrives on time):

7:00–7:15 P.M.	Welcome, news/reports/follow up from last week
7:15–8:05	Group's main activity (Bible study, discussion, and so on)
8:05–8:20	Prayer (as a group, individually, pairs, and so on)
8:20–8:30	Group administration (announcements, scheduling, and so on)
8:30	Adjourn (but people are free to stay and socialize)

Of course, this is only an example. Many variations are possible, and this particular example doesn't include who performs each agenda item. Nevertheless, using an agenda is a valuable vehicle to get you where you are headed and reach your meeting's objectives.

CHOOSING OBJECTIVES

During your review of the meeting's content, you need to select objectives. Once the planning process is well established in your thinking, you'll find yourself identifying objectives as you prepare the content. It's an acquired skill—something to practice and develop over time.

Objectives (aims, goals, or whatever term you wish to use) are intentional statements that translate your content into specific end results toward which your efforts are directed. They are written statements that provide direction, set the target, supply a path, and keep the group meetings focused. In other words, objectives identify what you want to accomplish by the time the meeting is finished. Unfortunately, objectives are too often assumed or even overlooked. The group leader just starts out with a vague sense of where he or she is going. This may work on occasion, but if you're serious about having great small group meetings, then it's mandatory to understand, develop, and use carefully crafted objectives.

I recommend written objectives. Why? Because writing them down forces you to think about what you want to do, why you're doing it, and how you intend to go about it. Besides, written objectives serve as records you can consult in the future to refresh your memory on what you've already attempted.

Objectives serve as essential planning tools. As such, and depending on the type of group you're dealing with, objectives can focus on "desired end results" that either reflect (1) meeting processes and procedures or, more importantly, (2) deal with specific dynamics you want to accomplish in your group members' lives. For example, "to cover chapter three" (a chapter on evangelism in a study guide) is a content or process objective, while "to identify a friend or relation you can share the gospel with this week" focuses on the group member.

Let's now consider some specific mechanics associated with writing good objectives. Here are six suggestions I want you to consider using.

First, objectives help you systematically identify what you want the group members to *know, feel*, and/or *do*.[2] Educational psychologists use the terms cognitive, affective, and psychomotor. More simply, the terms "know," "feel," and "do" are easier to remember and use. You'll recognize the key ideas associated with each term:

◆ Know = knowledge, facts, information, data, understanding, and insight
◆ Feel = attitudes, emotions, opinions, sentiments, and desires
◆ Do = actions, behavior, conduct, performance, activity, and presentation

Given your content, what do you want your group participants to know, feel, and/or do? It's possible, but not required, for every meeting to pursue objectives that focus on all three aspects. I know a group leader whose objectives structure his meetings this way. His first objective focuses on group members' biblical understanding (know). Brief lectures or "Bible discovery" teaching methods are used to familiarize the group members with the content. Next, he leads a discussion to explore the members' thoughts and attitudes (feel) produced by the biblical truth being considered. A carefully crafted objective guides these discussions. Last, he budgets time to pursue an objective that deals with possible individual and group actions (do) to apply the material. All this is done in about ninety minutes, including informal sharing and prayer. As you can tell, this process takes careful planning to do it correctly.

As an alternative, it's also possible to spend one whole meeting on each aspect; each week pursuing a different objective. For example, I was in a group where the content we studied permitted us to focus on facts/information (know) one week, discuss our reactions (feel) and possible applications (planning to do) the following week, and take corporate action as a group (doing) during the third week. Each new content area was approached using this three-week cycle. It was an invigorating experience because we took action together as a group (doing), not merely settling for individual efforts, during the third week.

Of course, you needn't include all three elements among your objectives. Selecting only one or two elements may better suit your group's overall goals, based on the type of group you're dealing with and on your specific objectives for any single meeting.

Second, in developing and writing your objectives, don't get hung up on their design and wording. Use syntax and words you understand. They are *your* objectives, not literary masterpieces to share with the world. The purpose is to guide your group processes and end results. You should know, however, some individuals advocate very strict methods for writing what they deem as "good" objectives. My advice is if you find a book or system to help you write objectives that makes sense to you, use it.

Third, since the intent is to write objectives you feel comfortable with and can use, consider the following guidelines:

◆ State your objectives using language that describes the
   participants' actions or attitudes. In my way of thinking,
   objectives that merely describe what you're going to do—a

process—aren't as beneficial as those that identify or describe
end results in your participants' lives.

◆ Use words that are precise and action oriented. For example, a
word like "understand" isn't as specific as the verbs "write" or
"describe." If a person can write about or describe something, it
usually means they understand. Conversely, if you use the word
"understand," how do you know if he or she really does
understand?

ACTION WORDS FOR WRITING OBJECTIVES

Words Open to Many Interpretations	Words Open to Fewer Interpretations
To know	To write
To understand	To recite
To really understand	To identify
To appreciate	To differentiate
To fully appreciate	To solve
To grasp the significance	To contrast
To enjoy	To list
To believe	To compare
To be aware of	To compute
To think	To state
To feel	

◆ After considering the previous two guidelines, write objectives
that identify conditions which tell you the objective is
accomplished. Some educators refer to objectives that manifest
this characteristic as being "observable" objectives. How do you
know or how can you tell when an objective is completed? In
part, how you write the objective and the words you use answer
this question. For example, how can you tell whether the
following objective is accomplished?

*Given a case study, group members will identify three violations
to the biblical expectations the apostle Paul sets forth in the
selected passage.*

Because this objective was written using an action verb ("identify"), which describes the group members' behavior, it can be clearly determined whether or not the objective is achieved; that is, the group members will be able to identify the three violated biblical principles (either verbal or written identification is possible). Furthermore, you can cite the specific Bible passage in the objective. If multiple objectives are being used, however, there is no need to include the passage in every objective. Besides, it's quite likely no one other than you will even see the objectives, and you already know what passage you're dealing with.

◆ Think about writing objectives that describe the conditions under which the group members' behavior takes place. Conditions are the limits or context in which the desired action or attitude is expressed. Conditions include instructions, problems, situations, physical settings, devices, events, behavior, or anything else that establishes the context or circumstances presented to the group members and/or under which they must act. For example, "Given a case study" is the condition of the written objective just given. Not every objective must include such a condition, but usually that kind of condition is more helpful when added. If you choose to include a condition in your objective, here are some suggestions to spark your creativity:

❑ Given six agree or disagree statements . . .
❑ Reading the biblical passage silently to themselves . . .
❑ Working with another group member . . .
❑ Without first discussing it among themselves . . .
❑ Before next week . . .
❑ Using a Bible dictionary . . .

◆ Aim at writing objectives that are short and to the point. Long and complicated objectives are usually more useful if they are rewritten as two or three separate statements, each focusing on one identifiable fact, behavior, or attitude.
◆ One last optional criterion. Consider writing objectives that establish how well the desired knowledge, attitude, or behavior must be demonstrated. In some cases it may be desirable to identify an expected performance standard. Phrases such as

"without any mistakes," "seventy-five percent of the time," "in ten words or less," "in correct order," or "within thirty minutes" all relate to how well something is done. Including a performance standard is often a good idea when writing objectives for task-oriented groups. However, this characteristic may or may not be appropriate for other types of groups.

Fourth, objectives for each specific group meeting must fit within the group's overall purpose or goals; that is, the primary reason for the group's existence. Your content and related objectives must promote the group's purpose. In practice this means writing objectives and doing things that are suitable for your specific kind of group. For example, asking members in a task-oriented group to share intimate personal details may be inappropriate. This fourth guideline is more abstract and difficult to apply than its companions, and yet I'd be remiss if I didn't bring it to your attention. Just keep asking yourself, "Does this objective fit into my group's purpose?"

Fifth, how many objectives do I need? It all depends; that is, how many objectives depend on your format and agenda. Some group leaders like a precise objective for each format element and/or agenda item. If this works for you, great! However, feel free to write only as many objectives as you think you need in order to focus your group meeting and direct your efforts. At very minimum, each meeting should have one central objective around which everything flows.

Finally, once your objectives are written, stay flexible. Some new group leaders make an error in assuming the meeting's objectives are fixed and no deviations are allowed. Wrong! Your objectives provide a road map, a plan, not a rut to follow. Stay alert to the Holy Spirit's leading. It may become necessary and appropriate to set your objectives aside and do something totally unplanned. Knowing when to do this is the trick. In chapter five we'll consider some guidelines.

DESIGNING ACTIVITIES AND METHODS

For many group leaders, maybe even you, it's easier to determine the meeting's content and objectives than it is to select appropriate activities, methods, or procedures to use during the actual meeting. Knowing "what" is easier than knowing "how." Nevertheless, having great group meetings depends on selecting and using activities and methods that accomplish your objectives.

What does a group do when it meets? How do I translate the content and objectives into meaningful activities in which the group members participate? Good questions. Unfortunately, there are no quick or simple answers. Selecting activities and methods isn't an exact science; it's an art. I can describe how you select an appropriate method, which I'll attempt to do in a minute, but in the long run, it's a skill built on experience. The more you do it, the better you'll become.

Before going any further, I need to make a distinction between activities and methods. While not totally distinct concepts, in my thinking an activity is the larger concept in which methods are used. For example, a Bible study is an activity that may utilize many different methods (such as lecture, discussion, and worksheets) to involve the group members. Usually you select a general activity and then the specific method. But wait! If this distinction doesn't work for you, just blend the two ideas together and use the words "activity" and "method" as synonyms.

On the next page is a flowchart designed to illustrate the method/activity selection process. Beginning with your content and concluding with a selection or decision, the flowchart depicts a selection process easier to describe than it is to do. It isn't a mechanical process. Like I said, it is more an art than it is a science.

Before we consider what the chart does and then how to use it by examining its components, let me explain the flowchart itself. The chart is an attempt to identify the various factors that go into selecting an appropriate activity or method. Please note I said "appropriate." An activity or method isn't "right" or "wrong," words that often convey moral or ethical dimensions. Rather, you need to determine if a potential method is *appropriate* or *inappropriate* to what you're doing. Therefore, our aim is to select appropriate methods.

The chart merely organizes and logically presents the issues you need to consider. It's a tool to guide your thinking. Beware: The logical sequencing may not always proceed as depicted. Often you'll find yourself piling all the factors together and considering them simultaneously, which is normal. In fact, the dotted lines on the chart's right-hand side—with arrows going both ways—is a "feedback loop" that represents this concurrent thinking, the interactive relationship between the selection factors. No one factor is the final decider, but working together they jointly help you sort through the options and select the best activity or method. Don't limit the flowchart to a rigid linear process. It's best if you view the process as a cumulative decision with each factor contributing to your final decision on whether or not to use a given method.

Six Elements to Selecting an Appropriate Activity or Method

Now let's turn our attention to the flowchart by reviewing each component in the logical sequence. But remember that the flowchart is only a tool. There is no magic. Instead, make any adjustments you think are necessary to suit your situation.

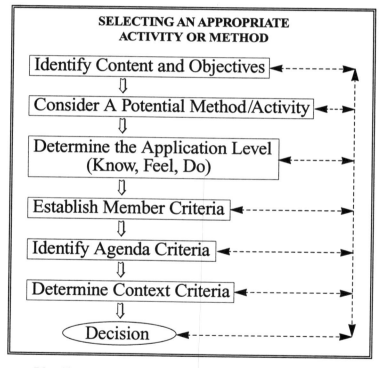

SELECTING AN APPROPRIATE ACTIVITY OR METHOD

Identify Content and Objectives

Consider A Potential Method/Activity

Determine the Application Level (Know, Feel, Do)

Establish Member Criteria

Identify Agenda Criteria

Determine Context Criteria

Decision

Identify content and objectives—As we discussed earlier, content is a central element in planning. Therefore, you must first consider your previously identified content and the related objectives you want to accomplish at the meeting in order to start off the method-selection process. Not all activities and methods work with every content area. Consequently, this means you need to identify which activities and methods are potentially suitable to your content. It's a judgment call on your part. The more you do it, however, the better you'll become.

EFFECTIVE METHODS FOR
BASIC APPLICATION LEVELS ARE:

KNOW   Focused reading, lectures, videos, field trips, exhibits, questions and answers, research projects, book reports, writing, demonstrations, games, sermons, drama, work sheets, paraphrase, case studies, interviews, panels, recordings, internet searches, library research, seminars, workshops, storytelling, charts, biblical word study, films, cassettes, and so on.

FEEL   Discussion, drama, art (such as mural, montage, mobile, frieze, collage, banners, and painting), pantomime, symbolic shapes, poetry, prayer, open-ended story, sentence completion, circle response, singing, sharing/listening, role playing, and so on.

DO   Demonstration, role playing, practice, drill, experiment, debate, field trip, prayer, visitation, work project, letter writing, skit, art, storywriting, practice teaching, photography, singing, playing a musical instrument, diary, drama, volunteerism, missions trip, telephone calls, interview, and so on.

Consider a potential method/activity—With your content and objectives in mind, what potential activity and/or method best fits the content and is most likely to help you achieve your objective(s)? The goal is to select an initial, tentative activity/method for further consideration. Ultimately you are attempting to match what you want to do with a method to do it. The biggest challenge for new group leaders is knowing what methods are possible. On the one hand, there are numerous potential methods from which to choose. On the other hand, there's always more than one activity or method you can use in reaching your objectives.

Although there are many activity/method options, don't despair. Go to your nearest Christian bookstore or your church library to get a book on small group methods, or, more likely, a book on teaching methods. Most teaching methods work well in group settings, but not always. Pick and choose carefully.

Determine the application level (know, feel, do)—When you wrote your objectives, perhaps you structured them around what you wanted the group members to *know, feel,* and/or *do.* Since each term represents a different application level, each requires different methods. Your aim is to decide if a potential activity or method is appropriate for the intended application level. For instance, if your objective is to help the group members learn to share their faith (do), a method such as role playing appropriately helps them practice the necessary skills. (See chart on page 35.)

Establish member criteria—Ideally, you know your group members fairly well. This is important. Knowing their characteristics, interests, likes, and dislikes plays a key role in selecting appropriate activities and methods. Younger adults (thirty-five and below) often like various kinds of activities while older adults (fifty-five and over) tend to prefer methods that are discussion oriented. Are these risky generalizations? You bet! I cannot tell you your group's "comfort level"—the degree or amount of discomfort. I know of only two ways to figure out your group's comfort level. First, ask them what type of activities and methods they prefer. Hopefully, they'll tell you. Second, try different methods and see what works. In most cases it takes both ways to discover the answer.

Identify agenda criteria—Does the method fit or work? Is it appropriate for your agenda? Does it require too much or too little time? A common mistake is to include too many activities and methods. Knowing how much time your agenda allows and the general categories included in your format are clues in helping you select your activity and method.

Determine context criteria—You also need to consider where the group meeting is held. Some methods require special equipment (overheads, projectors, open space, and so on) that may or may not be available at the meeting's location. Since most small groups meet in homes, you're wise to select activities and methods you know you can facilitate in this limited context. Don't make it hard on yourself. Be creative, but make certain any method you select is appropriate to your meeting place.

Decision—Having finally considered all the criteria, now it's decision time. Are you going to use the activity or method? Don't be afraid to decide. You might make a mistake once in a while, but in time your judgment will improve and you'll become a pro. Besides, no one will die if your selection proves inappropriate. There's always next time to improve. Just do it!

Six General Guidelines

In going through the process of selecting a method or activity, keep these six general guidelines in mind:

◆ An activity or method must focus the group members' attention and motivate them to participate.
◆ An activity or method must be explained so that group members understand what is happening and/or how they are being asked to participate.
◆ An activity or method must maintain the participants' ongoing interest.
◆ An activity or method is more effective if it isn't overused.
◆ An activity or method must enhance, not detract, from the content.
◆ An activity or method is only as good as the leader's ability to explain and use it.

ADDRESSING DETAILS

At this point you are continuing to pray, know your content, have written your objectives, and have selected the activities and methods you intend to use at the meeting. Now you need to determine what details are necessary to actually conduct the meeting. Normally, any details fit into three categories: people, place, and provisions.

People: Assigning Their Roles

Who is going to do what? Are you going to lead every activity or are other group members going to do something? Back when we discussed using an agenda to structure your meetings, I suggested "who" as an item often included in formulating an agenda. Someone must lead every meeting. There must be *a designated leader*. Usually it's the person who planned the meeting, but not always. Since you are doing the planning, I'll assume you're the designated leader. Even so, you may want to use willing group members to lead specific agenda items (prayer, sharing, the Bible study, singing, refreshments, and so on). Now is the time to identify those people you want to take on specific duties. Don't twist any arms. If a person isn't interested in helping, that's okay; just ask someone else.

After your group has been together awhile and developed "cohesion" (bonding, comfort level, "groupness"), you'll find the members more willing to participate. Therefore, don't be surprised if they are initially shy about participating. Go slowly. Ultimately, it's ideal to include as many people as possible in leadership roles (leading meetings or parts of meetings, as well as overall group leadership).

Place: Arranging the Setting

If your meetings are held at the same location week after week, the details associated with your setting don't take much consideration since you know what to expect. On the other hand, if your group meetings move from location to location (which I don't recommend), you need to make sure the setting is prepared. For example, is it set up and can it accommodate the planned activities? In my way of thinking, where you meet is as important as when you meet and what you do. Don't overlook your setting. The room arrangement, temperature, and lighting are also important and should be considered. Finally, be sure everyone knows where to meet.

Provisions: Identifying Needed Materials and Equipment

By "provisions" I mean the materials (paper, pencils, glue, books, Bibles, and so on) and equipment (video player, cassette recorder, and so on) you may need. You won't always need such provisions. Nevertheless, this is the time in your planning to identify what, if any, provisions you need to acquire and how to make the necessary arrangements.

EXECUTING FOLLOW-UP

The last planning step deals with several final tasks. First, you may need to follow up and do something you said you'd do at the previous meeting—purchase a book, call your pastor, or talk with an absent group member. Likewise, if you asked your group members to do something or come prepared to report on some activity, be sure to include whatever it is in this week's agenda. Second, make sure everything (people, place, provisions) is ready for the upcoming meeting. You may need to pick up something, make a few last-minute telephone calls to remind co-leaders, run off handouts, fix a dessert, or do whatever else is needed just prior to meeting. Once any needed follow-up is finished, you're ready to conduct the meeting.

The planning process for small group meetings may sound more difficult than you anticipated. Maybe, maybe not. Much depends on you, the time you invest in planning, and your previous experience with planning. If you're new to serving as a group leader, planning usually takes more time in the beginning. As you gain valuable experience, you'll find the process becomes easier and quicker. So hang in there and do your best. Remember the apostle Paul's words: "I can do everything through Him who gives me strength" (Philippians 4:13).

An Example

I tossed a lot of material at you in this chapter. Therefore, to conclude our discussion on planning, it's a good idea for us to work through an example to illustrate the ideas presented thus far. At the end of this chapter you'll find a filled-out planning worksheet based on a hypothetical meeting. A blank copy of this planning form is included. Use it if it works for you. If not, come up with your own.

TAKING ACTION

1. Describe your group's "format."

2. Outline your group's typical agenda.

3. Using the criteria presented in this chapter, write at least two objectives for your next meeting.

4. List where you can get ideas for group activities and methods.

5. Using the blank planning worksheet provided, plan your next small group meeting.

SMALL GROUP MEETING PLANNING WORKSHEET

Meeting Date: 14 May 199X   **Planner:** McBride

Planning Step	What	Who
PRAYER	Pray for the group members by name; remember Sue asked us to pray for her father, Ted, who has cancer.	Me
CONTENT	Chapter Six—Humility (Jerry Bridges, *The Practice of Godliness*, NavPress, 1983) Luke 18:14	Me
OBJECTIVES	By the end of this meeting members will be able to: ✓ Define biblical humility. ✓ Describe how a Christian practices true humility. ✓ Identify one thing they can do this week to practice humility.	Me
ACTIVITIES/ METHODS (AGENDA)	7:00–7:15 Welcome, News, Ask Beth about her job, Opening prayer	Chuck W.
	7:15–8:05 Bible study	Me
	8:05–8:20 Prayer in groups of three (Diane will explain)	Diane B.
	8:20–8:30 Group stuff—Ed (next month's group calendar)	Ed
	8:30 Adjourn—Remind them we meet at the Taylor's for the next three months.	Me
DETAILS	✓ Prepare a handout for the study. ✓ Make fifteen copies of the study handouts. ✓ Make blank calendars for Ed (sixteen copies).	Me
FOLLOW-UP	✓ Call Chuck, Diane, and Ed on Monday to remind them about their parts in the meeting. ✓ Ask the members to turn in their church directory information sheets handed out last week (must be in by Tuesday of next week at the latest). ✓ Turn in group meeting report to the church office.	Me

SMALL GROUP MEETING PLANNING WORKSHEET

Meeting Date: **Planner:**

Planning Step	What	Who
PRAYER		
CONTENT		
OBJECTIVES		
ACTIVITIES/ METHODS (AGENDA)		
DETAILS		
FOLLOW-UP		

CHAPTER THREE

Participation: Helping Everyone Become Involved

S mall groups are for people—all kinds of people. Frequently you'll find the only thing you have in common with new group members is your mutual status as brothers and sisters in Christ. Just meeting together on a regular basis may or may not transform the individuals into a functioning, effective group. It takes time, energy, and a good plan to help a collection of individuals become a real group and have consistently great meetings. Leaving this important process to chance isn't wise because great meetings happen by design, not default!

This chapter deals with how you, as a leader, can assist your group members in becoming active members and to fully participate and hopefully pursue total involvement—conditions necessary for experiencing great meetings. In my thinking, participation and involvement aren't the same thing. By the time you finish this chapter I think you'll agree. Before we tackle the difference, however, I want to share with you some foundational information undergirding participation and involvement.

PRACTICING WE, US, OUR

Have you noticed? The words *me, my*, and *I* are rampant in our culture. Christians are no exception; we frequently express this mind-set. Too often we limit our faith to "my" relationship with Christ, what God is doing for "me," or what "I" must do to apply God's Word. Such individualism is acceptable, but not sufficient. Our corporate identity in the body of Christ, the church, is also vital. The overarching goal, and your biggest challenge as a group leader, is to help the group become a group, to embrace and practice *we, us, our.* Helping them realize the joy and fulfillment associated with being Christ's body, our corporate identity and the responsibility we share as Christians, is an exciting adventure.

Helping a group become a true group is easier said than done. Yet being aware of the situation is a first step in the right direction. As group leaders we are better equipped to facilitate group development when we first know and understand the dynamics we are dealing with. Now let's investigate some of those foundational dynamics.

NOTING PEOPLE'S EXPECTATIONS

Perhaps the single most important dynamic you must confront early in the group's existence is the members' expectations for the group. Why do they want to be in the group? What do they hope to accomplish as an individual and as a whole group? Failure to identify and deal with members' expectations leads to problems later on if and when the group fails to satisfy one or more of the members' hopes, desires, or wishes.

Potential members evaluate the group and their possible ongoing involvement beginning with the first meeting. It's most often an unconscious, self-centered evaluation. Some objective logic is utilized, but usually it's the "feeling" they get from and about the group that either keeps them coming or closes the door to their involvement.

Expectations are key elements in this evaluation process. Every member comes to the group anticipating or expecting something—reasons that motivate them to "check out" the group. These stated and unstated expectations range from serious considerations to frivolous whims. Moreover, what is important to one member may have no significance to another.

Four Common Questions

Group members' potential expectations are too numerous to list all the possibilities. Nevertheless, here are four questions that reflect expectations I've encountered on a regular basis over the years. You'll rarely actually hear anyone ask these questions; usually people are too polite. Yet the attitudes and expectations reflected in the questions are quite common.

What's in it for me? We live in a "me-first" world. It's seldom any different in the Christian community. In fact, this me-centered expectation is the number one driver behind most people's motivation for being in a small group. It is not always a negative attitude. Nonetheless, this attitude reflects our society's preoccupation with self. "What's in it for me?" includes both spoken and unspoken needs, or conscious and unconscious motivations. We often are moved to action by experiences in our background we don't fully understand. Likewise, there are many social, spiritual, and psychological needs in our lives we do know about and seek to fulfill.

Looking on the positive side, we should note that group members might expect the group to assist in fostering their spiritual growth and development (a relationship group), to provide a context for Christian service (a task group), or to help them cope with an addiction (need-based support group). On the one hand, if the group fails to achieve their expectations, their willingness to participate in the group quickly diminishes. Yet on the other hand, if expectations are met, they are more inclined to continue and perhaps become significantly involved.

Do I fit? Everyone wants to fit in and feel comfortable. Rarely do individuals endure a situation where they view themselves as being the "odd duck." Thus a key expectation nearly everyone has is to feel comfortable among the group members—to feel accepted and appreciated. These are normal human desires.

Members must feel they fit in with the group if the group as a whole is to succeed. Great group meetings are possible only when the group members sense the other members want their friendship and respect their ideas and opinions. If this is lacking, don't be surprised if members quickly drop out. Therefore, you have two choices: Either form a group in which you know everyone will "click" together or develop a systematic strategy to help the members fit in and accept one another.

Do I want to do this? People tend to avoid doing things they don't know how to do or things that make them feel uncomfortable. In addition, most people have personal preferences that motivate their behavior. "I simply don't like this or that." It isn't a matter of right or wrong, but simply what the person likes or doesn't like to do. Therefore, if you ask them to do something they find objectionable, for whatever reason, it's likely they'll decline. If you keep asking, they may withdraw altogether.

Whatever "this" is, group members evaluate their continuing participation on whether or not they feel comfortable participating. This includes both the group's purpose and the group's actual activities. Members might initially come to the group but will seldom stay beyond the first few meetings if the group's purpose for existing entails something they don't want or don't feel comfortable doing. For instance, a person might initially come to a task group geared toward evangelism, but elect to drop out when she or he finds out the main evangelistic method the group is going to participate in is "cold turkey" witnessing in shopping malls.

What's it going to cost me? People always consider the cost—the time, energy, and maybe even the money (for curriculum, travel, ministry tools, and so on) it takes to participate. Some people don't want to spend much; they aren't willing to invest anything beyond the minimum. For others, cost is no object. They want and expect it to cost them something and are willing to make whatever investment it takes.

What does it "cost" to participate in your group? If you demand more than a member is willing to "pay," he or she is likely to withdraw. Consequently, it's very important to be upfront and clearly outline what it takes to participate in your group. For example, most people are especially concerned about time: "How much time will this take?" When asking individuals to join the group, I've found it best to tell them exactly what the group plans to do, as well as any spiritual, interpersonal, time, or financial expectations. Forthright honesty is always appreciated.

Can you think of any other expectations group members or you may have? I know I haven't listed all the possibilities. Be alert to other expectations you may encounter. But guess what? Expectations are like time; they change. Don't be surprised if just when you think you've nailed down all the prevailing expectations, the winds blow and everything changes.

Discovering Their Expectations
Now that you know about some key expectations your group members may have, how do you go about finding out their actual expectations?

1. *Ask them.* I've always found it beneficial early in the group's formation to invest time in discussing the group's purpose and the members' "hopes." My usual strategy is to spend the first three or four group meetings talking about the group's goals,

helping people to get to know one another, exploring expectations they have, and formulating a group covenant.

2. *Use a covenant.*[1] I know of no better tool to help you and your group deal with your expectations than a covenant. Moreover, a covenant is a great opportunity to clarify many administrative details, such as time, location, and agenda.

3. *Make it okay for members to have differing expectations.* Everyone doesn't have to think alike. However, if the expectation(s) differ greatly from what the group's purpose and goals are, it may be best for the person(s) to depart and find another group.

4. *Watch for signs.* Unspoken expectations that go unfilled are reflected in a group member's attitudes and actions. If you observe, for example, a change in a member's attendance pattern, declining participation in the group meetings, or an argumentative spirit, quite likely something is wrong. It may be a temporary struggle the person is facing, or it could be unmet expectations. The only way I know to clarify the situation and deal with it is to get together and discuss it one-on-one.

5. *Periodically ask them again.* Don't assume your group members' expectations remain constant from day to day. As already mentioned, expectations can change. Therefore, you're wise to periodically conduct a "formative evaluation"[2] to determine how things are going and if any adjustments are needed.

PROMOTING PARTICIPATION

Helping the individual members participate in the group is an early and ongoing requirement for the group leader. Active participation is a prerequisite to building an effective group and having great group meetings. By "participate" I basically mean regular attendance and actively taking part in group activities.

Four Prevalent Trends

Before I suggest some practical ideas on how to promote participation, let me share with you four prevalent trends that affect adults' participation in general. Pay close attention. You need to deal with all of these issues if you hope to have great group meetings.

Choices—Adults want and expect choices. We live in a society that affords individuals with many, many options when it comes to investing personal time, effort, and money. Doing it one way, limiting personal choices, or restricting options doesn't sit well.

I find people approach small groups with this same "choice" expectation. They want choices: the kind of group, when it meets, what it does, how long it meets, where the meetings are held, who the other members are, the amount of time it takes to participate, and how much effort they are going to invest. Consequently, and in the long run, if group members feel they have no say in matters and have no choice, they are prone to say "So long."

Convenient—Convenience is a big selling point. Just watch television. All kinds of products and services are offered as being quick, easy to use, and available everywhere. Few adults are willing to go out of their way; they expect, or at least prefer, whatever it is to be convenient and effortless. Only when confronted with this mind-set do they even realize they are operating in this fashion. Only then are they possibly willing to consider changing.

As much as possible small groups should be convenient. Most often this means selecting a time(s) to meet when people can participate. I frequently talk with individuals who say they cannot come because their work or travel schedule conflicts with the group's meeting time. Yet also keep in mind that this response may be an excuse. My experience tells me most convenience issues (excuses) are usually a smoke screen. The person espousing this logic just doesn't want to participate. But rather than being honest with himself or herself and you, the convenience justification is invoked.

Location is the other major convenience factor. Find a place to meet that is easy to find and as close as possible to a majority of the group members.

Meaningful—Adults need and want worthwhile, significant, purposeful activity. Gone are the days when people participated just because it was expected of them. Today adults aren't shy in saying no if they think the proposed activity—being in your group— isn't a potentially meaningful or beneficial experience. What makes it difficult is that meaningfulness is a fluctuating standard. Each individual makes the decision for himself or herself. And, of course, what is meaningful to one person often isn't meaningful to someone else.

Great meetings are viewed as being meaningful by most group members. While it isn't always possible, the majority must view the meetings as being productive and worthwhile most of the time. Should the members sense the group lacks purpose and/or significance, it isn't long before the group potentially disintegrates. This means you as the group leader need to plan and conduct meetings that fulfill this expectation. I know this sounds rather frightening, but it is a "burden" all group leaders must accept. But you can do it! Don't let one or two picky members or a few dud meetings derail you.

Questioning—Today questioning everything is inherent in our democratic society. Many older adults were taught not to question authority or anything else. But all this changed after World War II when questioning became ingrained in our educational system. I attended college in the sixties. The emphasis was on "questioning" more than on "knowing" facts. Today this mind-set continues. We feel comfortable calling into question everything and everyone. It's "normal."

Expect your group members to question everything. After all, it's their "right," or so they feel, to examine, object to, or doubt anything you say, suggest, or do. Don't take it personally. On the contrary, when they question what's going on, it's a fairly sure sign they are interested and willing to participate in the group's development. In fact, on occasion you might find it profitable to set aside some time in a meeting to answer any questions the group members have about anything affecting the group.

How to Encourage Participation
Promoting and building active participation among your group members takes time and effort. Rarely does it just happen. Consider all these possible actions:

1. *Invite their participation.* Don't just assume they are on the same wavelength with you. Spend time in group meetings talking about the group's future and how every member's active participation is key to its success. Ask them to join you in making the group worthwhile.
2. *Talk with individual group members outside the group's regular meetings.* Get together for a cup of coffee or some other informal activity. Ask their opinion on how the group is going and what

they think you can do to help the members actively participate. If you think they might be receptive, ask for their help.
3. *Look for ways to help members participate.* As the group develops greater comfort with you and one another, begin using group activities that facilitate the members' interaction. Try asking select members to do small but specific tasks, such as lead in prayer, make a group calendar, call group members, plan a social event, or lead part of the meeting.
4. *Recognize their participation.* Genuine verbal praise is an effective means to reinforce past participation and encourage future participation.

MAINTAINING INVOLVEMENT

How is involvement different from participation? Good question. Although participation comes first as a foundational component, it may or not may lead to active involvement. I use the word "involvement" to describe a group member who emotionally buys into the group and accepts the opportunity to play a more active role in leading the group and helping it to succeed. Moving beyond regular attendance and taking part in group activities, this member becomes committed to the group and dedicated to its well-being and success. Not all group members reach this level. It's possible to actively participate without becoming involved. In fact, some groups never require, expect, or ask for more than simple participation.

Let me make another comparison. The difference between participation and involvement is similar to the distinction between dating and getting married. Dating is participation while marriage is involvement. Just as not all dating leads to marriage, participation may or may not lead to involvement.

My experience tells me only three or four out of twelve group members become truly involved. These few individuals eagerly move from participation to active involvement. They willingly assume key roles in helping the group succeed, such as leading group meetings, attending leadership training, planning and conducting a meeting, recruiting new members, helping other members participate, monitoring group norms, representing the group at church leadership meetings, looking for ways to help the group improve, and zealously talking about the group. All these activities, and potentially others, reflect more than the activity itself. More importantly they demonstrate the members' commitment to the group, to other group members, and to small groups ministry in general. Of these three or four involved group members, normally only one or two totally "buy" into small group ministry's big picture. These group members frequently become group leaders themselves, and some even wind up as proven leaders for the overall groups ministry. They're sold on how important small groups are and enthusiastically want to participate in advancing the ministry. I look for these folks. They are the ones who keep small groups going and growing.

How do you move a person from participation to true involvement? There aren't any guaranteed methods or tricks, but let me suggest some ideas (similar to the suggestions I gave earlier to encourage participation):

1. *Invite their involvement.* Don't wait for them to come to you to bring up the subject. Spend time in group meetings talking about involvement opportunities and how all members are eligible. Tell them how to go about becoming involved.

2. *Talk with individual group members outside the group's regular meetings.* Get together for a cup of coffee or some other informal activity. Encourage them to consider a more committed involvement. Tell them why you think they in particular should explore the possibility of becoming involved.

3. *Look for ways to help members increase involvement.* As you get to know the individual group members and discern which ones may have an interest in being involved, begin asking them to do specific tasks that require more time and effort.

4. *Recognize their involvement.* A short, personal thank-you note is an effective means to reinforce past involvement and encourage future involvement.

5. *Encourage them to assume leadership.* After a member has taken the initial steps leading to greater involvement and has shown the desire and willingness to learn, be bold and suggest they consider leading a group themselves. If they agree, help them take the necessary steps required in your church, such as training, internship, and assistant leadership, in becoming a group leader.

USING ACTIVITIES AND TASKS TO BUILD GROUPS

Most groups, especially relationship groups, need to budget time during their early meetings to participate in group-building activities. The purpose is to help the group become a group, not just leave the process to chance.

Numerous resources exist to help you select or design group-building activities You may want to find others, but at least check out the three I list below.

◆ Johnson, David W., and Frank P. Johnson. *Joining Together: Group Theory and Group Skills.* Englewood Cliffs, NJ: Prentice-Hall, 1987.
◆ Coleman, Lyman. *Youth Ministry Encyclopedia.* Littleton, CO: Serendipity, 1985. (This book contains very useful ideas for adults as well.)
◆ Griffin, Em. *Getting Together: A Guide for Good Groups.* Downers Grove, IL: InterVarsity, 1982.

REACHING OUT TO ONE ANOTHER

The phrase "reaching out to one another" may sound mushy, but back in the sixties I heard this term used a lot, and it's still relevant today. It conveys the idea of people seeking to connect with one another in spiritual and emotional dimensions. Such is the case in small groups.

Small groups serve their ideal purpose and succeed only when all the members accept their individual and corporate responsibilities as group members. In reaching out to one another, the members view the group as an opportunity to "do" church, practice biblical Christianity, and be the body of Christ. It's an exciting and mutually beneficial process.

In the final analysis, participation and involvement in small groups means brothers and sisters in the Lord reaching out to touch one another's lives and reaching out to experience God's blessings. You, as a small group leader, play a key role in this process by planning and conducting great small group meetings.

NOT FORCING IT

I conclude this chapter with one final piece of advice: Don't force it! You can do everything within your power to help the group members fit in, participate, and become significantly involved . . . and still some will ignore you. Remember the old saying: "*You can lead a horse to water, but you can't make it drink.*" People aren't horses, but the idea still holds. Twisting arms or shaming people rarely works. And if it does, the results are usually hollow and fleeting. No, you simply can't force people to participate in groups or coerce a collection of individuals into becoming a group or into having great meetings. All you can do, with God's help, is try.

Take courage! Keep trying! "Commit to the LORD whatever you do, and your plans will succeed" (Proverbs 16:3).

TAKING ACTION

1. Rate your group's "we, us, our" status (circle a number on the continuum).

   Just Starting   Fair   Good   Excellent

   1   2   3   4   5   6   7   8   9   10

2. What expectations do your group members have? How do you know what they are? How does your group deal with these expectations?

3. What percentage of your group members are participating versus truly involved?

   _____% Participation

   _____% Involvement

4. List three things you think you can do to increase your members' involvement.

5. What did you do, or plan to do, to help your group become a group?

CHAPTER FOUR

Variety:
The Spice of Life

Whoever said, "Variety is the spice of life," understood that as humans we need diversity in our lives. Doing the same thing day after day, constantly repeating activities and procedures, often leads to another saying: "Familiarity breeds contempt." Do you think variety is necessary for your small group meetings? Most likely, you do.

If you're like me, habits form quickly. I don't mind new situations, but after a short time I figure out the system, whether it be a new job, committee, school course, sport, or just a task. Meanwhile, I form attitudes and behavior patterns that become comfortable and easy. Group meetings often follow this same path. After a while we find meeting formats and procedures that are comfortable and easy to repeat. We settle in and potentially fall into a common trap—just doing it without giving it any thought. It then becomes a habit.

Habits aren't necessarily bad. In the case of routine group meetings, however, when habits are left unexamined, group meetings can easily sour and become unproductive. Great meetings are dependent on this malady *not* happening.

What's your "variety quotient" (VQ)? Just as your IQ measures your intelligence, your VQ measures your ability to handle or tolerate variety. This chapter is designed to assist you in examining your VQ. But don't panic! VQ isn't something you can fail, nor is a low score an indicator that you lack leadership skills. It will, however, alert you to ways in which you can make your meetings even better.

Picture in your mind VQ existing on a continuum. At one end, a high VQ means you enjoy and prefer lots of variety—the more diversity the better. At the opposite end, a low VQ indicates intolerance or dislike for variety—constantly doing the same thing is preferred. Most people aren't on either end, but fall somewhere in between the two extremes.

Unlike IQ, however, VQ lacks a value orientation. A high VQ isn't "good," and a low VQ isn't "bad." Both high and low VQs are acceptable. Some group leaders with low VQs are able to plan and conduct excellent group meetings, while some high VQers tend to overdo it and kill their groups with too much or inappropriate variety. The real goal is to understand and use variety as a key element in having great group meetings. A balanced approach to variety is facilitated, in part, by discerning both your own VQ as well as your group members' VQs.

How do I measure my VQ? Although there aren't any valid and reliable instruments that can measure your VQ, I do provide a rating scale for you in this chapter's "Taking Action" section. But first, we need to define those terms that relate to variety.

UNDERSTANDING VARIETY

Like most words or ideas, variety can mean different things to different people. It's probably a good idea, therefore, to define what I mean when I use the word. Within a small group's context, "variety" means avoiding constant uniformity, offering a reasonable mix of suitable agenda options, and using an assortment of activities and methods in your group meetings. Meanwhile, variety does *not* mean using the same methods, procedures, or activities over and over again.

Naturally, variety is linked to selecting activities and methods (see chapter two). It's a vital relationship. Variety serves as another important standard or criterion guiding the selection process. Not only do you need to know how to select appropriate activities and methods, but also you need to create an appropriate mix that includes variety. Nevertheless, it's impossible to have a suitable mix without knowing what activities and methods you can vary. Variety *demands* alternatives. Numerous activities and methods are at your disposal. The only limitation you face is your knowledge, understanding, and skill in selecting, mixing, and using the methods.

APPLYING VARIETY

Using variety in your group meetings is possible on several levels. First, there is variety in the overall group format—the meeting's main activity. Let's say you lead a need-based group—for sake of discussion, a divorce-recovery support group. For weeks each meeting has focused on allowing the participants to vent their frustrations, share victories, and pray for one another. Why not bring a little variety to the next meeting by asking the members to focus on helping someone? Have them select an older widow in your church and volunteer to do her spring cleaning, do yardwork, cut wood (assuming she has a fireplace), or invite her and her friends out to lunch. You might find a complete change in activity has an invigorating effect on the group. For this to be effective, remember that how you "sell" the idea is just as important as the idea itself.

Second, vary any lesser activities on the meeting's agenda. Other than the group's main activity, such as a Bible study, change the group's other minor routine activities. For example, if every week your agenda includes prayer, think about occasionally replacing prayer with worship, praise, or even singing. This isn't to suggest you don't pray at all, but not as a routine group activity. Of course, you can also vary your other agenda activities.

Third, consider using variety *within* various meeting activities. Going back to our previous example about using prayer, try various methods within this activity. One group I was in budgeted time each week to pray together. In addition, we explored prayer from many different vantage points. We prayed individually, as a whole group, in pairs, men with men and women with women, standing, and kneeling. Furthermore, before we prayed, we often spent a few minutes examining a select Scripture passage to learn something new about prayer. Prayer was the activity on the agenda, but variety in our methods kept it fresh and interesting.

Fourth, vary the time. If your group meets weekly for ninety minutes, schedule one or two longer meetings every quarter. Use the extra time to evaluate your progress as a group, complete tasks that demand more than your normal time, or do anything else you believe will benefit the group. What's more, variations in time naturally fit and work with any variety in terms of the activities and methods you may plan.

Another time variation is the amount of time you allot for each agenda activity. You may normally plan twenty minutes each week for prayer. Why not add a little variety once in a while by increasing or decreasing how much time you plan for this and other important group activities?

One more time idea. Add some spice to your meeting schedule by changing the day and/or time you meet. However, adopt this idea with reservation. Many group members have fairly rigid personal and work schedules that are difficult, if not impossible, to change. Changing the meeting time may cause more trouble than it's worth. Yet it is an option to investigate.

In general, when it comes to using variety in time, proceed with caution. If your group members are like mine—very busy people—popping a time change on them isn't appreciated. It's smart to announce any planned time variations one or two meetings in advance. Doing so allows the members to adjust their schedules, if necessary, and their plans to participate.

Fifth, my last suggestion is for you personally. Consider some variety in *your* small group leadership experience. Try leading a different type of group. If you're an experienced group leader but all your experience is with task groups or relationship groups (the most common), then it may be time for you to lead another kind of group. Of course, changing group types isn't mandatory, but this experience may expand your vision for groups, teach you a few new skills, and open up whole new opportunities you never anticipated.

In addition, variety can be conventional or unconventional—that is, selecting and using activities and methods in your meetings that are known, accepted alternatives compared with options that are unfamiliar and perhaps even "daring." In my current group the members probably would join me in kneeling as we pray together. It would be interesting, however, to see their reaction if I asked them to prostrate themselves (lay on the ground face down) as we prayed to our living God. The point is that kneeling is both unusual and conventional. Whereas, prostrating ourselves is more than unusual; it's downright "weird," or at best uncomfortable, to most Christians.

In summary, the correct use of variety keeps your group meetings fresh and vital, thus avoiding a situation in which group members trudge along doing the same thing time and again. It means planning and conducting meetings that include a well-thought-out mix of activities and methods. These are the kind of meetings members look forward to attending and feel are significant to their lives. Indeed, these are the kind of meetings that are great!

AVOIDING THE FAMILIAR RUT

So what's the bottom line when it comes to variety? The object is to keep your meetings creative and stimulating and to avoid producing and following a familiar, easily convenient "rut" or groove. I've attended many "mindless" meetings where the members just go through the motions. Sadly, too often they didn't even know they were in a unproductive rut. Is your group in a format, activities, or methods rut?

How do we elude ruts? We've already talked about varying the group's activities and methods. Another strategy in avoiding the familiar rut is to vary the pace or tempo of the meeting. Pace is how fast the group meetings move along, the tempo at which group activities are accomplished. Some groups are slow and plodding in their meetings. Nothing happens quickly, and they accomplish very little. Other groups operate at a frenzied pace: go, go, go! There's little time to stop and catch your breath. Either extreme is just that—an extreme. Most groups find a pace somewhere in between and then stick with it without ever making it an issue.

What's your group's pace? Perhaps you should try to slow down or speed up your group's agenda at different times. Varying the pace can allow you to accomplish more. Perhaps you'll even be able to smell the roses if you slow down now and then. For example, one group set out to cover one chapter per week in their study guide. The members found they were rushing through the material at times and missing key points. They decided to change their pace and spend two or even three weeks on a chapter in some cases. This slight adjustment in the tempo of their meeting produced more learning and higher satisfaction among the members. (We'll discuss pace again in chapter six when we consider the leader's role as a model.)

As we get older, our tolerance for change diminishes. We become comfortable and secure in familiar routines. Our ruts become something we count on. We like those familiar customs in our lives. Small groups are no different. Over time the individual members, and the group as a whole, tend to lean toward replicating and maintaining familiar patterns. Is this tendency wrong? It certainly is not. Nevertheless, plodding along in ruts frequently prevents us from fully discovering and enjoying what it means to meet together in small groups as Christian brothers and sisters.

"I never thought about it" is a common response when I ask leaders whether or not their small group is in a rut. You, as well as all other small group leaders, need to think about it, particularly now that you are aware of the benefits variety can give to your meetings.

DEALING WITH TOO MUCH VARIETY

Keep in mind this common rule: *Too much of anything isn't good.* Variety in your group meetings is no exception to the rule. It's easy to go overboard and use variety to an excess. Wanting to keep things fresh and lively is good, but finding the right balance can be quite tricky. Why? Because there is no universally true criteria for making this important determination. The type of group, its members, your skills, the setting, how long the group has met together, individual member characteristics, as well as numerous other factors, all interact and produce potentially hundreds of different combinations while affecting everything about your group, including variety. Like many other dynamics you must deal with them as a group leader. It's really your call. Time and experience are your best allies in this elusive but achievable process.

A popular fairy tale comes to mind. Goldilocks found Papa Bear's chair too hard, Mama Bear's too soft, but Baby Bear's "just right." Finding a "just right" variety level demands sensitivity and experimentation on your part. As with Goldilocks's experiences, there may be some "breakage" along the way, but don't give up. In addition, you're wise to remind yourself that variety isn't a final state or condition one finally reaches but an ongoing dynamic to constantly pursue.

The amount or level of variety you find acceptable may or may not be suitable to the whole group or the individual members. Some people may like considerable variety. Others may prefer little or no variety. They want to keep it like it is—have it stay the same. It's possible you might have a high VQ while your group or individual group members possess low VQs. If this is true, finding the right balance becomes even more arduous, but you have to keep trying. It's worth your time and effort.

TAKING NOTE OF VARIETY GUIDELINES

Using variety in a correct manner is a challenge. While no simple formula exists, here are some guidelines that may help you find the correct balance for you and your group:

1. *Use variety as a flavoring or spice in your group meetings, not as a staple.* As previously mentioned, shy away from too much or too little variety in your group meetings. Ignoring this advice, some leaders use so much variety it becomes the focus of the meetings, and then meetings become a circus. Rather than allowing variety to spice up the meetings, variety becomes so dominant that it changes the group's flavor altogether and overpowers the main course. To illustrate my point, think about salt. Used in the right amount, salt enhances the flavor of food and makes food more enjoyable. Too much salt, however, overwhelms the dish and masks the flavor. "It's too salty" replaces "Mmmm, good!" Moreover, no one I know sits down to a meal consisting entirely of salt. Salt is a spice, not a main course. Likewise, variety fits this same logic.

2. *Remember the group's purpose and goals.* It's possible to get so infatuated with variety that you begin using methods and activities that don't fit the group's reason for existing. The aim for variety is to use appropriate activities and methods that enhance and promote the specific kind of group you're leading.

   The four types of groups (relationship, content, task, and need-based) introduced in chapter one don't necessarily require specific activities and methods. Many alternatives are suitable for any kind of group. Yet, as you make your selection, be sure to keep in mind its goals and why the group exists, and put together a variety mix that fits. How to do this is up to you. The basic questions you must answer are:

   ◆ Is this activity/method suitable for what the group is attempting to accomplish?
   ◆ Does it complement or work with the other methods I intend to use?
   ◆ Have I used it too often lately?

A "yes" answer to the first two questions, as well as a "no" to the third, triggers a green light for you to go ahead and give it a try.

3. *Be sure group members know what's going on.* Variety can sneak up on people. When you use new activities, they see that things are being done differently, but they have no clue as to why. To ward off any potential problems that may arise because group members aren't clued in, be sure you explain what you're doing. If they know why you're using a variety of activities and methods, it's more likely they will go along with you. Since there are no guarantees, however, proceed with caution. Choose your words and actions well.

4. *Stay within the group's "comfort level."* I mentioned this concept in chapter two when we discussed selecting methods. To refresh your thinking, "comfort level" denotes using activities and methods in which the group as a whole or individual members feel comfortable participating. This same principle extends to variety.

Prostrate prayer, the illustration I used earlier, is definitely outside most Christians' comfort level. If this fact is true for your group, you would do well not to force this prayer method, or any "more than unusual" method, on your group members without first discussing it with them and securing their consent.

You can increase your group's variety comfort level by going slowly and not forcing the issue, as well as observing the other guidelines listed here. Just remember how you feel when you don't like or appreciate doing something that is unfamiliar. Likewise, don't think your group members are any different. Invite them to talk about their comfort level. It's a healthy way to address the issue and build a common understanding and acceptance among group members.

5. *Move from the familiar to the unfamiliar.* Unless you have a really unusual group, it's fairly certain that your members won't jump from familiar, comfortable group activities to ones they consider unconventional in a single leap. It takes time to introduce variety to the group's agenda. This is especially true if your group members are older and have been doing the same

things for a long time. The best strategy is to slowly introduce variety. "Slowly," by the way, is different for different people, and for different groups. What may seem excessively slow to you quite likely might be too fast for some group members.

6. *Look for alternatives.* As previously mentioned, variety demands options. There is no way you can develop good variety in your meetings' activities and methods without first knowing your options. Keep your eyes and ears open. Ask what other leaders are doing. Read. Attend small group conferences. Explore every opportunity or avenue you can take in building your activities/methods repertoire. Every activity or method you come across may not fit your group, but maybe you can share it with another leader who leads a group in which it might work.

7. *Allow group members to suggest alternatives.* You're wise to include your group members in selecting and/or approving the group's activities. At first, they may be slow in making any suggestions, but don't lose patience or give up soliciting their insights.

8. *Find a balance everyone, or at least the majority, can live with.* This ideal standard is much easier to suggest than it is to follow. Unfortunately, you may never achieve the perfect balance when it comes to variety. Nonetheless, it's worth an attempt. Just remember not to expect everyone to agree. It's a rare event when all group members totally agree on your variety mix, or anything else for that matter.

9. *Ask for feedback.* As with everything the group does, it's wise for you to seek feedback from the members. Call it evaluation or whatever you like, but invest some time in seeking the members' opinions on your group's variety level. What activities and methods do they like and dislike? Are we doing too many things or too little?

   Feedback is usually gathered by informally talking with the group members or by using a formal method, such as group discussion or a survey. Incidentally, formal methods frequently include questions about other issues besides your activities/methods variety. (For further help, check out "formative evaluation" and endnote two in chapter three.)

10. *Last, expect to make a few flubs . . . We all make them!* No one
    is perfect. As you attempt to find the right methods and
    activities, and then organize them into a workable mix, you'll
    make a few mistakes along the way. It's normal. Therefore,
    don't get impatient with yourself, the group, or the process.
    Besides, there is no perfect, absolutely inviolate variety standard
    you must achieve. Some weeks your meetings will be super—
    just the right variety of activities and methods. Other weeks
    you'll wish you could rewind the clock and reclaim the wasted
    time. Be prepared to laugh at yourself, and invite the other
    group members to join you. The road to great meetings gets
    bumpy on occasion.

Now that you know more about variety than you ever thought
you'd know, what's your personal and the group's VQ? The following
TAKING ACTION section is designed to help you answer this question.

TAKING ACTION

1. No valid instrument exists to measure your VQ (variety quotient).
   Therefore, rate yourself on the following 1 to 10 scale: 1 meaning
   no tolerance for variety; 10 meaning a preference for abundant
   variety. Remember, there are no right or wrong answers.

   No Variety   Some Variety   Abundant Variety
   1   2   3   4   5   6   7   8   9   10

2. How would you rate your group's overall VQ?

   No Variety   Some Variety   Abundant Variety
   1   2   3   4   5   6   7   8   9   10

3. List possible alternatives for putting variety into your group
   meetings.

4. Is your group stuck in any "ruts"? If so, what can you do to
   change the situation?

5. Reviewing the variety guidelines presented in this chapter, list
   any additional guidelines you think are necessary given your
   situation and group.

CHAPTER FIVE

Spontaneity: Following the Spirit's Lead

Put down this book right now and go buy yourself an ice-cream cone. Did you do it? No, not very spontaneous, are you? Or at least silly suggestions do not entice you, right?

When it comes to small groups, like people, some are spontaneous and some are not. I'm sure you know individuals who are inclined one way or the other. For a few folks, spontaneity is an evil to avoid. Others, especially the creative types, earnestly proclaim its benefits. Most people, however, don't have a strong opinion either way. Their reactions to being spontaneous depend on the circumstances at hand. Sometimes they like it, and sometimes they don't. This same diversity in opinions applies to spontaneity within small group meetings.

Are great small group meetings *planned* meetings? Of course they are—at least that's what I've argued in the four previous chapters. While not wanting to violate my basic assertion, I must spend a few pages exploring with you how to use spontaneity in your group meetings. This is an interesting twist because being spontaneous seems like the exact opposite of planning. Not necessarily. Besides, as we'll see, a measure of spontaneity prevents your group meetings from becoming rigid and inflexible, especially spontaneity motivated by the Holy Spirit.

Here are the questions we need to answer: When is and isn't spontaneity appropriate in small groups? How does or doesn't spontaneity assist in having great meetings? At the risk of being redundant, I say there are no easy answers. It all depends. At times spontaneity in small group meetings is appropriate, but at other times it isn't. In this chapter we will investigate when it is and when it isn't, and how to know the difference.

UNDERSTANDING SPONTANEITY

Before going any further, we need to define what we mean when we use the term "spontaneity." It is important to define key terms. That way everyone tracks together. Therefore, let's spend a few minutes defining and understanding "spontaneity." *The American College Dictionary* provides the following definition of the word:

spon-ta-ne-ous, *adj.* 1. proceeding from a natural personal impulse, without effort or premeditation; natural and unconstrained: a spontaneous action or remark. 2. (of impulses, motion, activity, natural processes, etc.) arising from internal forces or causes, or independent of external agencies. 3. growing naturally or without cultivation, as plants, fruits, etc. 4. produced by natural process.

"Spontaneity," as a noun, means the "state, quality, or fact of being spontaneous." These definitions provide us with good clues on how spontaneity fits into small group meetings.

On the surface, it would seem spontaneity by definition violates careful planning. But does it? Are the two apparently opposite ideas—planning versus spontaneity—mutually exclusive? Does one negate the other? Is there no place in planned meetings for impulsive, unpremeditated, unconstrained, spontaneous actions or remarks? In answering these questions, let's examine the definition of "spontaneous" a bit closer to glean a few ideas.

First, spontaneity is demonstrated in action and/or by remarks (that is, behavior and/or words). As a group leader, you can rarely restrain a group member's comments or actions, but you do have the ability to influence or control the group's corporate actions—what the whole group does. There is a difference between an individual group member acting or speaking in a spontaneous manner and the group as a whole being spontaneous and doing something a group member, or even you, suggests at random.

Since dealing with individual spontaneity is a topic for group dynamics, not planning great group meetings, I am going to limit our discussion to group behavior—the group as a whole acting spontaneously. The spontaneous actions or remarks of individual members can certainly influence a meeting's dynamic and outcome, but this is really a subject for another book.

Second, spontaneity is a natural, personal impulse. Our human spirit is creative, inventive, and fanciful at times. We often are whimsical in our actions and speech, sometimes without thinking. Likewise, a group can possess these same qualities, except the impulse for potential group action must originate with an individual member. You or a member may respond to the moment and spontaneously suggest that the group do something or even go somewhere. When this occurs, we must, of course, determine whether or not the "impulse" is from the Holy Spirit's leading, an issue we'll examine shortly.

Third, being spontaneous happens without effort or premeditation and is produced by natural process. Certainly we can plan time for the whole group to brainstorm or be creative, but a meeting isn't spontaneous if it is planned. However, it is possible to set an atmosphere for the meeting that allows and nurtures spontaneity if and when it occurs.

Fourth, no criteria to determine spontaneity's "quality" is included in the definition. In other words, the definition doesn't put a value on being spontaneous. Nothing is said about spontaneity being "good" or "bad." This is correct in my thinking. Being spontaneous is like selecting a group activity or method; it's better to think about it being "appropriate" or "inappropriate." (Nevertheless, keep in mind that on rare occasions spontaneity may produce a "bad" outcome that can be quite hurtful to a group member or the group itself.) Deciding whether spontaneity is appropriate or not is usually easy to determine, but at times it may not be.

Fifth, the definition says nothing about two functional issues: context and time. By "context" I am referring to *where* appropriate spontaneous actions (and comments) occur. Meanwhile, "time" speaks to *when* it is appropriate and for what *duration* of time. In short, spontaneity isn't limited to approved places at certain times for set time lengths. It can happen anywhere at anytime during small group meetings. Yet, just because it *can* happen, doesn't mean we must *always* permit it to take place. Controlling or managing spontaneity in your group meetings is essential.

Spontaneity within group meetings may change the meeting's

entire direction, add an unplanned event, or just derail the group for a few moments. These possibilities may be appropriate and may not be. It depends on the situation and the group. Nevertheless, appropriate spontaneous actions or activities may take little, some, or all of the group's time.

APPROPRIATE SPONTANEOUS ACTIONS AND ACTIVITIES

This chart does not come close to listing all the appropriate spontaneous actions or activities. The following examples, however, represent alternatives that are typical and may occur spontaneously (unplanned) in group meetings:

Actions

✓ Stopping to pray
✓ Verbal praise to God
✓ Lifting up hands in praise
✓ A Christian hug

✓ Breaking out in a chorus or song
✓ Holding hands
✓ Reading a biblical passage
✓ Getting a cup of coffee

Activities

✓ Singing
✓ Prayer
✓ Going out for pie
✓ Adjourning

✓ Visiting someone in the hospital
✓ An entirely different task
✓ Any other unplanned group activity that fits the group's purpose and goals

---

Sixth, our definition doesn't state or even imply that spontaneity is random, unexpected chaos. This is important. While it may happen despite your efforts, being spontaneous doesn't mean irresponsible, haphazard behavior. Instead, spontaneity may be rightly characterized as thoughtful, responsible actions. This is especially true if you are aiming at having great small group meetings. You should certainly discourage any inappropriate spontaneity to occur during your meetings. (We'll look at this issue again later in this chapter where I list for you when spontaneity is and isn't appropriate.)

One more idea about group spontaneity not connected with the definition. Your group's purpose and goals help determine how much, if any, spontaneity is appropriate. Different types of groups either lend themselves to spontaneous action or mitigate it. For example, task groups tend not to be spontaneous by nature. After all, they exist to accomplish some specific job. Spontaneous actions that deviate from the task are unproductive. Conversely, need-based groups thrive on being spontaneous. Appropriate unplanned actions, in keeping with the moment, are valid and may in fact be inherent to the group's purpose. You cannot always plan in advance how you respond to a need, especially if you don't know what needs may be expressed.

EXAMINING WHAT THE BIBLE HAS TO SAY ABOUT SPONTANEITY

You might already know that Scripture says nothing specifically about being spontaneous. Nevertheless, there are several biblical passages I believe are helpful in shedding some light on our topic.

First Corinthians 14:40

"But let all things be done properly and in an orderly manner."
(NASB)

I often cite this favorite verse when I talk about planning. Paul is referring to exercising spiritual gifts, which have spontaneous qualities in this passage. Yet in doing so, he sets forth a universal principle to govern everything we do. Applied to our topic, a proper and orderly manner must characterize your group's spontaneous actions or activities. Random uncontrolled or unproductive actions or activities are out. Spontaneity must proceed with order and in a proper manner. Later, I will give you my personal "bottom line" when it comes to spontaneity. In that upcoming section I suggest what proper and orderly spontaneity looks like.

Second Corinthians 5:14

"For the love of Christ controls us." (NASB)

Love—God's love for us and our love for God and one another—is a central theme in Scripture. It is a standard for us to apply in all our relationships. With God's help your group is a bastion for expressing and experiencing genuine biblical love. Therefore, any and all spontaneous actions and/or activities must comply with and promote this biblical mandate. Love is the controlling factor, an underlying foundation, for everything the group does . . . planned or unplanned.

Proverbs 25:28

"Like a city that is broken into and without walls is a man who has no control over his spirit." (NASB)

This verse speaks to individual group members. Spontaneous activities aren't the opportunity for me, you, or any other group member to go unchecked and do or say anything we please. Unbridled words or behavior reflect poor self-control. We must exercise personal responsibility and control ourselves. It's difficult at times, but doing so demonstrates Christian maturity. My spontaneous actions in or suggestions to my group also fit this expectation.

Proverbs 16:9

"The mind of man plans his way, but the LORD direct his steps." (NASB)

Remember this important verse! Both planning *and* divine direction are necessary. You are responsible to carefully plan your group meetings, but it is ultimately God who directs our steps. We must remain sensitive to being directed by God even after everything is well planned. Just as the Holy Spirit can lead you as you plan your meetings, He can also redirect your plans once the meeting is underway. Remain open to the Holy Spirit's direction and sensitive to His guidance. This is such an important issue that I want to address it more thoroughly in the next section.

DISCERNING THE HOLY SPIRIT'S LEADING

I'm sure you are familiar with the phrase, "guided by the Holy Spirit." To me this means doing what the Holy Spirit wants by seeking to discern the Spirit's direction and making divinely guided decisions. We quickly recognize the Spirit's guidance in our individual lives, but why are we much slower to discern or promote His working in our corporate lives? Nevertheless, I'm convinced the Spirit works in the whole group as much as He does in the lives of individual group members. Understanding this dynamic is important to having great meetings.

Once again we need to turn to God's Word and examine how it applies to small groups. Unfortunately, Scripture doesn't offer an easy formula to determine the relationship between spontaneity and the Holy Spirit. Yet, among many possible biblical verses, here are three key verses found in Galatians to assist us in our quest for understanding this issue:

Galatians 3:5

"Does God give you his Spirit . . . among you?"

Just as we believe the Holy Spirit "indwells" (lives within) individual Christians, we can also acknowledge His presence in our corporate midst. We can correctly maintain that the Holy Spirit lives within each of us as a person and among us as Christian group members. In other words the Holy Spirit lives within the group as a whole through the indwelling of its members. One could even make a case for suggesting the Spirit's power is potentially greater within a group context—that is, a group of believers has a greater cumulative effect of the indwelling Spirit's presence.

Galatians 5:16

"So I say, live by the Spirit."

Since we possess the presence of the Holy Spirit in our lives, the natural reaction God expects from us is to follow the Spirit's lead. Our mutual goal is to live in the Spirit's power and operate within His control. Again, this requirement is true for both individuals and small groups alike. After all, the small group is the body of Christ in a tangible form. Hence, not only the individual group members, but also the group, functioning as a group, must live by the Spirit.

Galatians 5:25

"Since we live by the Spirit, let us keep in step with the Spirit."

Several ideas are important in this verse. First, note the word, "since," makes an assumption about us as Christians. It assumes we now live in the Spirit's control. Second, the words "we" and "us" denote our mutual relationship with God's Spirit. Being in a small group also makes this relationship physically real to us. Third, "keep in step with the Spirit" tells us to stay tuned, keep connected, march to His beat. Like soldiers, we organize ourselves in an orderly manner and march in step to the Spirit's drumbeat. If you have ever seen soldiers march, you know a platoon marches much better together than an individual soldier marching alone.

I think it's possible to view spontaneity—at least in part and in its best sense—as the group responding to the Holy Spirit's leading. If this is so, and given the biblical passages we just reviewed, how do we determine whether or not God's Spirit is suggesting a spontaneous action or activity? Determining "how" is not an easy task. Nevertheless, I suggest several practical possibilities based on my experiences (quite possibly you may have additional suggestions):

◆ It's quite possible that the call for spontaneous action is from the Spirit if *everyone* senses it is the right thing to do. More than a mere feeling, I'm talking about an "inner assurance" in which all of you "just know" it's the thing God wants the group to do.

◆ Quite likely the Holy Spirit is motivating this suggestion if it promotes a biblical passage you are studying or if it glorifies Jesus Christ.

◆ If the suggested activity spiritually edifies the group members, the source for this spontaneous suggestion is surely the Holy Spirit.

◆ Perhaps it is the Holy Spirit's leading if the spontaneous behavior complies with one or more statements listed in the section, "When to Deviate from Your Plan," which we will discuss later in this chapter.

If you can't affirm one or more of the above possibilities, does it mean the suggested spontaneous action or activity is *not* the Holy Spirit's leading? Possibly, but it is advisable to avoid dogmatic statements that restrict the Spirit's methods. Nevertheless, these suggestions should go a long way in helping you discern the Spirit's leading.

APPLYING SPONTANEITY

Personally, I favor what I call "controlled spontaneity" in small group meetings. This means the group leader encourages spontaneity within established boundaries and leads the group in correctly responding to spontaneous remarks, actions, or suggestions group members make during a meeting. Moreover, I suggest you plan *for* spontaneity, not *plan* spontaneity.

How to Plan for Spontaneity
I believe planning *for* spontaneity involves the following three things:

Encouraging spontaneity—I like to encourage the group to welcome spontaneity as a positive element during the group's meetings, understand it as a tool for keeping the group energized and dynamic, and view it as one way the Holy Spirit works within the group. Of course, as with all good things, it's open to abuse. Therefore, the group needs to discuss the matter and arrive at what they determine is and isn't acceptable spontaneity within their group meetings.

Acceptable spontaneity—The group must decide if and what type of spontaneity is acceptable in their group meetings. Is all spontaneity okay or is none permissible? (The latter is extremely difficult, if not impossible, to enforce.) Or is there an acceptable midpoint on the spontaneity continuum? What spontaneity boundaries are agreeable to all the members? How is this determined?

One workable idea is to discuss spontaneity at some point during the initial meetings when your group is first forming—perhaps when you formulate your group covenant (some authors use the term "group contract"). The members may want to include a section on spontaneity in their written covenant identifying the acceptable parameters in which it may occur. Trying to identify specific behaviors, actions, and activities as being appropriate or inappropriate may be unnecessary, however. Attempting to do so may take too long and make the covenant far too lengthy. A better alternative is to stipulate some general guidelines (boundaries, expectations) to govern spontaneity, similar to those presented below:

◆ Spontaneous comments, behavior, and suggestions for group actions and activities are welcome, but members are responsible to control themselves in these matters.

◆ All spontaneity must be edifying; rude behavior or disrespect for other group members is unacceptable.

◆ Fellow group members are expected to respond to suggested spontaneous actions or activities in an accepting manner; the member making the suggestion shall graciously abide by the group's decision.

Dealing with spontaneity—Remember the biblical standard we identified earlier: Do all things in a proper and orderly manner (1 Corinthians 14:40). Keep this in mind as your underlying principle. It must guide how the group responds when a member spontaneously suggests the group do something. More importantly, the goal is to remain sensitive to and follow the Holy Spirit's leading.

Early in the group's existence the leader may need to take the lead in responding to suggestions by asking the group what they prefer to do. A vote or some similar formal decision-making process isn't usually necessary. General comments or nonverbal cues (heads shaking, facial expressions, and so on) are often sufficient to discern the group's mind. Furthermore, don't be afraid to ask the question, "Is this God's will for us?" Seeking a group consensus normally takes only a few minutes, if that long. In some cases you may want to pray before making a final decision.

On occasion a suggested spontaneous activity may generate strong feelings and, perhaps, some heated discussion. When this occurs, be sure to remain calm as you deal with the situation and apply our underlying principle. When strong divergent opinions arise, it's usually best to set spontaneity aside and stick with the original meeting plan. Likewise, I never proceed when the group is split over the suggestion. Acting spontaneously based on a simple majority vote isn't a wise move.

As the group develops increasing "groupness" (cohesion and comfort with one another), other members may respond to the suggestion first and lead the group in making its decision. Likewise, in some cases, depending on the person, the individual making the suggestion can help the group evaluate the spontaneous activity and determine whether or not it's the Spirit who is leading the group to proceed or set the alternative aside.

On occasion there is no need to discuss the proposed spontaneous behavior. It just happens and everyone participates. For example, the other day a member in my group was sharing a difficult situation he was facing. Spontaneously another member invited us to join him in praying for our brother. As you can imagine, we eagerly joined in without discussing whether we should or not.

Appropriate and Inappropriate Examples of Spontaneity

Since we've talked at considerable length about spontaneity up to this point, let's tie things together by looking at four examples, which may be useful to illustrate what I see as appropriate group spontaneity.

Example One—Carol is upset; her divorce is final tomorrow. The task group had planned to complete their current project that evening. Instead, the leader suggests they set aside their work and spend the next hour talking and praying with Carol. Everyone quickly agrees.

Example Two—The group has been studying the idea of Christian service for the past six weeks. As the leader that evening, you're all prepared to lead the group in considering the next chapter in your study guide. As you just get started, Sarah, the church secretary, suggests the group put into action what they are learning by going to the church office and helping her put together the church directories, which she hopes to mail tomorrow afternoon. After a few minutes discussing the idea, the group concurs and heads off to the church.

Example Three—During the scheduled worship time, Ted stands and lifts his hands in praise. Silently, the other group members, one by one, also stand and join Ted in lifting their hands to God.

Example Four—Frank doesn't feel like participating in the planned discussion this evening. He suggests to the other members they all go bowling and just enjoy being together. The group members' reactions are mixed. After they discuss the pros and cons and pray about it, all but Frank and one other member feel it wasn't a good idea. In the spirit of unity, Frank and the other member cheerfully accept the group's decision.

So what do you think? What's your position? Does spontaneity fit into small group meetings? If you answer yes, read on to learn more. If no, skip the rest of this chapter and proceed on to chapter six.

When to Deviate from Your Plan

Knowing when to permit or even encourage spontaneous behavior is not an easy task. Lord willing, the guidelines suggested below can assist you in determining when spontaneity is appropriate in your meeting. Ideally, one or more of these conditions should exist before you deviate from your planned meeting to pursue a spontaneous alternative:

◆ When a group or a member's need is recognized and can be addressed in a better fashion by deviating from the plan and doing something you or another group member suggests
◆ When the suggested activity is a better method to achieve your meeting's objectives
◆ When the group members agree to the spontaneous activity or method
◆ Whenever the suggested action better promotes the group's purpose and goals
◆ Of course, most importantly, when the group members and you are convinced the Holy Spirit is calling you to do something

When NOT to Deviate from Your Plan

I'm sure you can come up with additional guidelines on when spontaneity isn't a good reason to deviate from your planned meeting, but here are some guidelines I use:

◆ If being spontaneous means acting in an uncontrolled manner
◆ When the spontaneous activity potentially causes spiritual, emotional, or physical pain for one or more group members

◆ When there isn't a consensus among the group members to proceed
◆ If the spontaneous activity exceeds available time and/or other available resources
◆ When the suggested activity is in conflict with the meeting plan and might potentially derail the meeting altogether if it were done
◆ If the suggested activity doesn't fit your group's purpose or goals

Since You're Spontaneous, Now What?
We've already determined that being spontaneous is acceptable and at times even desirable. Now we need to deal with the aftermath from being spontaneous and determine what to do since the meeting plan was abandoned.

Setting aside your plan has consequences. In task groups spontaneity may mean having to retrace your steps and come back to finish the project at another time. Or if your group is part of a larger small groups ministry where all the groups are doing the same thing, you may find your group out of sequence and behind. Although spontaneity may be desirable and motivated by the Holy Spirit, spontaneity may result in circumstances that you'll need to address and work out.

Specific results from being spontaneous are hard to predict. The possibilities are limitless. Consequently, it's hard to suggest the exact steps you need to take in dealing with the potential "fallout." You could encounter circumstances I've never experienced. So, my best advice is twofold: first, talk about it—have the group members discuss what took place and determine the best response alternative(s); and second, don't get uptight—sometimes there is nothing you can or need to do in response, meaning the best response is merely to move on.

To wrap up this chapter let's return to the two questions we posed at the beginning: When is and isn't spontaneity appropriate in small groups? How does or doesn't spontaneity assist in having great meetings? You can implement the answers you learned in this chapter as you do the following TAKING ACTION section.

TAKING ACTION

1. In your own words, describe spontaneity in terms appropriate for small groups.

2. Thinking about your group, describe any spontaneous activities the group did within the past three months.

3. Scripture is our basis for planning and conducting great meetings. List any other relevant verses you think add to the discussion in this chapter on what the Bible says about spontaneity or the group's responding to the Holy Spirit's direction during group meetings.

4. Answer the two basic questions in your own words: When is and isn't spontaneity appropriate in a small group? How does or doesn't spontaneity assist in having great small group meetings?

5. Thinking about your own group, describe an instance when you thought it was good for your group to act in a spontaneous manner.

CHAPTER SIX

Modeling:
Setting the Example

An insightful educator once said, "More is caught than taught." It's certainly true for small groups! Your group members "catch" your example and attitudes much quicker than what you teach and tell them. Put simply, as a small group leader, you are a model whether you like it or not. The responsibility comes with the job. Group members watch how you handle yourself during group meetings and, in general, how you live day by day. Consciously or unconsciously they are asking themselves, "Can I pattern my life after this person?" Does that frighten you? Don't run off because you think being an effective model is impossible. You can do it!

In this chapter I will share how you can succeed in setting a worthwhile example for your group. Doing so cannot be planned, per se, but being alert to the dynamics involved is an important first step. By the time you finish reading this chapter, you'll have the necessary confidence you need to do an outstanding job as a leader-model. Great group meetings are definitely in your future.

MODELING THE APOSTLE PAUL

Small group leaders are wise to adopt a mind-set and actions demonstrated by the apostle Paul. He fully understood the leadership role. Indeed, I'm amazed at his bold declarations. Talking to the Christians in Corinth, he made a rather startling statement: "I exhort you therefore, be imitators of me" (1 Corinthians 4:16, NASB). When is the last time you heard a Christian leader make such a pronouncement? It just doesn't happen very often. So-called "Christian humility" (or in reality the inability to make such a claim) prevents us from encouraging others to follow our example. After all, we aren't worthy is our meek claim. Too bad we, unlike Paul, are hesitant or simply feel we cannot invite others to emulate our lives. Ah, but we can! It is possible with God's help, some knowledge, and a workable plan.

Let's invest a few minutes in examining Paul as a model and see what we can learn from him. Five important insights come to mind.

Paul Accepted His Role as a Model

Paul acknowledged and embraced his role and responsibility as an example for other Christians to follow. His acceptance, however, wasn't because he was a terrific fellow. Rather, he understood that his task was to model and reflect God's character. In fact, he once again told the Corinthians to imitate him, but a condition is added: "Just as I also am of Christ" (1 Corinthians 11:1, NASB). Paul understood that his imitating Christ was essential and served as the real basis for others to follow his example. He simply told the Ephesians to "be imitators of God" (Ephesians 5:1). Paul laid open his life for others to follow because His overall purpose was to serve God and make the Lord known.

As a small group leader, you are a model. Just like Paul, you need to accept the fact that being a leader means having people watch and hopefully follow your example. Lord willing, your life is worthy to copy because you join Paul in seeking to imitate Christ (Galatians 2:20). Only as you are totally tuned in to Jesus Christ can the Holy Spirit produce in your life anything worth emulating. We—you and I—cannot do it on our own.

Paul Encouraged His "Group Members" to
Follow His Example

Wait! The word "encouraged" may be too mild. In fact, Paul "demanded" it when he said to the believers in Corinth, "I exhort you" (1 Corinthians 4:16, NASB). He didn't assume or hope the Corinthians would follow his lead; he boldly commanded them to do so. In fact, Scripture records at least five instances in which he not only offered himself as a model, but also expected them to follow. Indeed, Paul wasn't timid in his straightforward admonition to the Philippians: "The things you have learned and received and heard and seen in me, practice [a present tense imperative in the Greek] these things" (Philippians 4:9, NASB).

You may not have Paul's boldness when it comes to asking your group members to follow your example; few people do. Nevertheless, it is acceptable to do so if you are asking them to see and practice Christ living within you. Any other basis for inviting your group members to follow your example isn't acceptable.

Let's quickly consider how you can ask the group members to follow your example. The easiest way, of course, is not to ask at all and hope they somehow "pick up" on your example. This might work, but it makes the whole process uncertain. A better alternative is to *offer* yourself as an example. Explain to the members that you see your responsibility to them as one that includes living a life in Christ which they can follow with confidence. Don't make any wild promises or claim perfection. Just tell them your goal is to model for them, with God's help, a growing, vital Christian life—with all its ups and downs. If this initial strategy meets with success over time, then just like Paul, someday you may confidently invite them to imitate you.

Paul Led as a Servant-Leader

Paul understood that genuine Christian leadership entailed being a servant. Jesus Christ had previously set the standard by leaving heaven, assuming human form, and then dying for all mankind (praise God He arose from the dead and lives today). Now that's servanthood! (see Mark 10:45.) Paul sought to follow Christ's leadership style in every respect. Consequently, he assumed Christ's servant attitude and methodology. Paul summed up his willingness when he declared, "Though I am free and belong to no man, I make myself a slave to everyone, to win as many as possible" (1 Corinthians 9:19). What an awesome statement, especially when you consider it came from a man who was highly educated and a former member of the Jewish religious elite. Not at all typical or expected, but that's the beauty of it.

The servant-leader model doesn't make any sense to some people, particularly nonChristians. It runs contrary to our society's thinking. Servants, not leaders, serve. Yet it's important for us to remember that servanthood in the body of Christ is a high calling. Moreover, serving one another is an expected practice among all believers (see Galatians 5:13). As a small group leader you set the example in fulfilling this expectation. One caution is necessary, however. We serve one another as Christ's slaves doing God's will from the *heart*. We do it gladly. We should also keep in mind what Paul told the Ephesians, "With good will render service, as to the Lord, and not to men" (Ephesians 6:7, NASB). Let's not forget we serve God by serving others.

Nevertheless, what does being a servant-leader mean on a functional basis? Paul gives us some insight based on his own experience with the Thessalonian Christians:

> For we [Paul, Silvanus, and Timothy] never came with flattering speech, as you know, nor with a pretext for greed—God is witness—nor did we seek glory from men, either from you or from others, even though as apostles of Christ we might have asserted our authority. (1 Thessalonians 2:5-6, NASB)

Paul was comparing his "style" with certain dubious characteristics commonly associated with many leaders in his day. These same negative traits are still rampant among many contemporary leaders. Although other inappropriate servant-leader traits are listed in Scripture, I will cite what Paul noted as the four negative characteristics, which should NOT distinguish a true servant-leader:

◆ A servant-leader doesn't use flattery to manipulate people.
◆ A servant-leader isn't greedy; he or she isn't in it for personal gain.
◆ A servant-leader isn't interested in receiving glory.
◆ A servant-leader doesn't assert his or her authority.

Paul Didn't Claim Perfection

Paul was human. As such, he wasn't perfect and didn't pretend he was or make any such claim. On the contrary, Paul talked about his flawed human nature in his letter to the Romans when he described how he struggled with sin (Romans 7). He labored under no delusions about his status. He even referred to himself as the worst of sinners (1 Timothy 1:15) and "the very least of all saints" (Ephesians 3:8, NASB). Nevertheless, Paul's humility didn't prevent him from telling the Philippians to "join with others in following my example" (Philippians 3:17).

Being a model for your group to follow doesn't demand perfection.

Like Paul, you are human; you have flaws. But also like Paul, neither is your humanity something that disqualifies or prevents you from living a life worthy of imitation. Your worth as a leader and a Christian example isn't found in your humanity, in your skills and abilities, but in your status as a new creature in Christ (2 Corinthians 5:17). You operate in God's power (Ephesians 3:7), not your own. "For it is God who is at work in you, both to will and to work for His good pleasure" (Philippians 2:13, NASB). Exciting, isn't it!

Paul Acknowledged His Love and Care for Those He Served
Wrapping up his first letter to the Christians in Corinth, he said, "My love to all of you in Christ Jesus" (1 Corinthians 16:24). From prison, Paul wrote to the Philippians to tell them "how I long for all of you with the affection of Christ Jesus" (Philippians 1:8). Instructing them to "stand firm in the Lord," he called them "my brothers" and "dear friends" and disclosed his strong feelings for them by referring to them as "you whom I love and long for, my joy and crown" (4:1). Likewise, Paul knew there were some individuals among those he ministered to and cared for who shared mutual feelings toward him. He asked Titus to "greet those who love us in the faith" (Titus 3:15).

An interesting side note: We don't know if Paul by nature was warm and affectionate *in person*. We do know, however, his writings are filled with strongly expressed concern and love for people. I'm especially impressed by his words to the Thessalonians:

"We proved to be gentle among you, as a nursing mother tenderly cares for her own children. Having thus a fond affection for you, we were well pleased to impart to you not only the gospel but also our own lives, because you had become very dear to us." (1 Thessalonians. 2:7-8, NASB)

Paul used strong word pictures in this passage—words that convey important traits associated with being a model (servant-leader):

◆ A servant-leader is a gentle and caring person.
◆ A servant-leader builds close, affectionate relationships.
◆ A servant-leader imparts (shares, gives, entrusts) his or her own life.

I don't know about you, but these qualities are hard for me. Being a loving person doesn't come easily. Nevertheless, you and I must openly express Christian love to our group members. Words alone aren't sufficient. Our attitudes and actions must demonstrate care and concern. And yet, similar to everything else associated with being a Christian servant-leader model, we cannot be loving like Christ on our own. As "imitators of God," we are told to "walk in love, just as Christ also loved you" (Ephesians 5:1-2, NASB). Only then can we properly channel God's love to our group members.

How do you model love and concern? Different small group leaders do different things. There is no one way to model genuine biblical love. Find ways with which you feel comfortable. Here are some rudimentary ideas. You'll catch on quickly. I left several blank checks at the end so you can add your own suggestions.

- ✓ Help them paint their house.
- ✓ Take them out to breakfast (lunch, coffee, and so on).
- ✓ Visit them in the hospital.
- ✓ Admit it when you are struggling with God's will or a decision.
- ✓ Offer to take or pick up their kids.
- ✓ Give genuine verbal praise.
- ✓ Look for "silent" ways to encourage (a card, flowers, a handwritten note).
- ✓ Baby-sit for free.
- ✓ Ask for help.
- ✓ Take chicken soup to them when they are sick.
- ✓ Tell them you are praying for them.
- ✓ Share your prayer requests.
- ✓
- ✓
- ✓
- ✓

This concludes our brief journey in exploring what Paul (via the Holy Spirit) can teach us about being a model. Lord willing, it provided you with some basic ideas about your modeling responsibilities as small group leader. Now it's time to translate your knowledge into action.

SETTING THE GROUP ATMOSPHERE

Great small group meetings require a caring, supportive atmosphere—one in which the members feel comfortable and know it's "safe." To a large degree, especially early in the group's life, you are responsible to foster a healthy group atmosphere by modeling permissible attitudes and behaviors. The group may discuss the issue when you develop your group covenant, but then it's only theory put on a piece of paper. How you talk and behave translates the covenant into "flesh and blood" and sets the group's true atmosphere.

When talking about small groups, the word "atmosphere" refers to the spiritual, emotional, and relational climate (environment, aura, feeling, mood) existing within the group. Note I use the word "existing." This is intentional because every group has a healthy or unhealthy climate. In physical terms we use the word "weather." Here in Nebraska, where I live, a phrase such as "Wow, it's cold!" is routinely used to describe the weather outside. Similarly, we can describe the climate or weather inside a group. Many common weather phrases also aptly describe a group's climate. Do the following phrases sound familiar to you?

- ◆ "It's sunny and warm"—a pleasant, caring group
- ◆ "It's hot"—stress is high among group members
- ◆ "It's cold"—the group lacks personal warmth and acceptance
- ◆ "It's humid"—a stifling tension exists
- ◆ "It's storming"—members strongly disagree or are ranting and raving

Guess what? You are the group's weather forecaster. That's right! You're responsible for the group's atmosphere in two ways: First, you must "read" your group's climate. Sometimes it's easy; other times it's not. You may not be good at it at first (I wasn't), but it's a skill you can develop and master over time. Second, unlike your favorite television meteorologist, you must help *create* the climate in your group and continue to re-create the atmosphere each time the group meets. Sound fun? Actually, it is enjoyable to see your efforts produce a pleasant, productive group atmosphere. So let's get on with it and look at these two atmosphere issues more closely.

Reading the Weather

Wait a minute! How does reading the group's "weather" relate to this chapter on modeling? The answer is simple. You cannot be certain you are modeling the right attitudes and behaviors required for a healthy group atmosphere unless you are able to read the results. It's like a conductor/composer who doesn't know how to read or write music but is attempting to lead the orchestra. Once in a while this person can fake it and produce fairly decent results. But over the long run the lack of skill becomes painfully apparent. Such is the case for a group leader who doesn't possess knowledge and skill in discerning the group's climate.

You must know the options in order to decipher the group's atmosphere. This isn't as easy as it sounds because literally thousands of alternatives exist. Each possibility represents a different level or combination of four components or conditions: (1) spiritual, (2) emotional/psychological, (3) relational, and (4) physical. When combined, these components produce the group's atmosphere. Let me quickly explain each condition and offer you some tips.

Spiritual—A group's spiritual climate encompasses its purpose, the members themselves, and the emphasis placed on spiritual matters or issues. To begin with, every Christian small group, regardless of type, is a "spiritual" group. The Holy Spirit indwells all believers (see chapter five), and subsequently He is present at every group meeting. Yet every small group may not have the same spiritual emphasis within its meetings. Task groups usually place less focus on spiritual issues when compared with relational or need-based groups. Content groups can go either way; some emphasize spiritual matters while others don't. Furthermore, the group's spiritual climate usually mirrors the individual members' spiritual maturity. When group members are "mature" believers (assuming more than merely how long they've been Christians), the group tends to reflect this spiritual status. Of course, the opposite is also true. Newer Christians often lack spiritual maturity, and thus their groups do likewise.

Discerning the group's spiritual atmosphere may include (1) members talking about God's will, biblical principles, and so forth; (2) biblically acceptable responses to frustrating and/or difficult situations; or (3) their praying together. If these or other similar indicators are missing or occur infrequently, you may have a spiritual climate problem.

Emotional/Psychological—Both the individual members and the group as a whole contribute to the emotional atmosphere existing within the group. We must not forget we are created by God as emotional/psychological beings. Denying this reality can give you some big headaches. Similar to spiritual maturity, your group members also have varying levels of emotional well-being. Diversity is normal. You'll find most members are emotionally "balanced," and you'll experience no more than the usual ups and downs associated with life. On occasion, however, you may have a member or two who lack stability in this area. Such individuals can put a tremendous strain on the group. More significantly, when the group has three or four emotionally immature members, it can result in a dysfunctional group.

Emotional maturity in people is evidenced, for example, by the ability to disagree without being disagreeable, by a willingness to compromise, by not becoming angry over petty matters, by reacting appropriately to stress, by putting others ahead of oneself, and by listening to other's opinions. Don't expect perfection in these and other related issues. Any normal group member has good and bad days. Likewise, this is true for the whole group.

Relational—Relationships are the glue holding a group together. Ideally, everyone in your group likes, appreciates, and accepts one another. Unfortunately, the ideal isn't always true. Over the years I've been in very few groups where *everyone* gets along well. It seems as if there are always one or two members who don't "fit," for whatever reason, or are unable to build solid relationships with the other members. Usually there is nothing you can do about it other than keep trying to facilitate opportunities for the members to establish mutually beneficial friendships. We can love each other in the Lord, but not necessarily like each other or want to spend our free time together.

Reading the group's relational atmosphere involves watching to see how the group members treat and talk to each other. Healthy relationships mean the members are kind, courteous, helpful, and verbally encouraging to one another. Another indicator is how much time, if any, members spend together outside the group's regular meetings. It's a fairly safe bet your group has a good relational climate if the members "hang out" together in other social contexts.

Physical—While it's the least important atmosphere component, nevertheless, the physical setting in which the group meets makes an indispensable contribution to the group's climate. The room's literal climate is important. Rooms that are too cold or too hot detract from the meeting's success. Other considerations, such as furnishings, size, and orderliness also affect the atmosphere.

A group's physical atmosphere is the easiest element to determine . . . just look. Are there physical characteristics or conditions present that enhance or detract from the group's functioning properly? The wise small group leader pays attention to and then does whatever is necessary to enhance the group's physical setting.

KEY QUESTIONS FOR "READING" THE GROUP'S ATMOSPHERE

Here are some key questions you can ask yourself and the other group members in an attempt to discern the group's atmosphere (and represent issues you can model):

Spiritual
1. Do group members talk comfortably about spiritual matters?
2. Do group members pray regularly with one another?
3. Are group members active in seeking biblical lifestyles?

Emotional/ Psychological
4. Are group members able to disagree without being disagreeable?
5. Do group members have healthy self-images?
6. Are group members open to constructive criticism?

Relational
7. Do group members linger after the meetings to talk?
8. Do group members spend time with each other outside group meetings?
9. Do group members turn to each other in dealing with difficult times?

Physical
10. Does the group meet in a "comfortable" location?
11. Is the setting prepared for the meeting?
12. Are there environmental issues needing your or the group's attention?

Some people are good at discerning the group's climate but are clueless about how to go about effecting a positive influence. In being a good small group leader, you need to know both how to read *and* how to create your group's atmosphere. So how do you do it?

Creating the Climate

When it comes to creating your group's atmosphere, your task is twofold: (1) attempting to plan the atmosphere and (2) modeling the appropriate attitudes and actions that build a positive group climate. Let's revisit the four atmosphere components, but this time, we'll focus on planning and modeling.

Spiritual—Planning your group's spiritual climate, as with planning all the atmosphere components, is done while attempting to identify and provide conducive activities, methods, and experiences. Taking into consideration your group's purpose, plan meetings that establish and promote spiritual growth and honesty. It does no good for your group to fake spiritual matters. Be sure to tell the members it's perfectly acceptable to admit spiritual struggles and ask for assistance. This requirement is especially true for need-based and relational groups.

As the group's leader, you must portray what spiritual maturity is. Some group members, especially new believers, are looking to you to help them understand spiritual dynamics. You can, of course, explain many things, but your life is the best way for them to *see* God at work. Sure, this is a big responsibility, but don't forget what you learned from the apostle Paul's example. Like Paul, you needn't be afraid to encourage people to follow your example if you are modeling genuine, biblical Christlikeness.

Emotional/Psychological—Setting emotional boundaries early in the group's existence is the best way to plan the group's emotional atmosphere. This boundary setting is usually done when you formulate your group covenant. By establishing clear norms (see pages 46 and 55 in *How to Lead Small Groups*), the group determines what personal and interpersonal behaviors are acceptable. Doing this doesn't mean you won't have a problem or two, but at least you have a basis for addressing the matter should it arise. In addition, make it clear that emotional outbursts by group members will bring a response from you, and perhaps in the future other group members, in an attempt to deal with the situation.

You need to display emotional maturity. Your example sets the tone. When you model emotional/psychological stability, the other group members are likely to follow your pattern. But understand me correctly! I'm not talking about hiding your problems and struggles. Doing so violates your bond with the other group members. Instead, I'm talking about responsible emotional honesty, which is a valued commodity. Furthermore, always "spilling your guts" isn't any more desirable than it is to "clam up" and share nothing. Your emotional risk taking with the group begins slowly at first and increases as the group builds relationships and trust.

Relational—Nearly every group I've been in invested time in establishing relationships between the group members. I cannot think of any group where relationships between the members aren't important. You can facilitate this important dynamic by planning specific activities that assist the members in getting to know one another. Some group leaders spend the first three or four group meetings allowing the members to "tell their stories." Fun activities are used—within and outside the group meetings—to help the participants relax and enjoy one another's company. Some groups are designed to foster "deeper" relationships. Once the members know one another on an informal, factual level, the leader introduces activities that require sharing more personal, intimate information. The type of group and its purpose dictate whether "deeper" relationships are appropriate or not.

Once again you set the example. If you model an open friendliness toward group members, they are likely to respond similarly toward you and their fellow members. Every group member needs to view you as their friend—someone they can trust and turn to in joyous and difficult times. Quite likely you won't have this ideal relationship with all group members, by their choice, but you at least need to model a willingness on your part. One caution, however. Be careful about becoming too exclusive in your relationship with any one group member, especially members of the opposite sex, at least to the point where the other members feel you are ignoring them and favoring this one person, or persons. Some argue Jesus had a "favorite"—John ("the disciple whom He loved" referred to in John 19:26, 20:2, 21:7), but Jesus was God after all. I'm not saying don't have close, personal friends. My advice is to just be careful about your group relationships. You don't want to model favoritism or exclusivity.

Physical—As I said before, the physical setting in which the group meets must not be overlooked. Plan to arrive early and make certain everything is prepared. It may mean moving some furniture, helping the hostess fix coffee, picking up the kids' toys, or anything else you can do to create a warm, orderly environment. Some meetings may require planning for unique locations, arranging the room in a different way, or even bringing some special equipment or supplies that affect the physical atmosphere. Remember, planning for the physical atmosphere is among the necessary details associated with planning great meetings.

I can imagine you're wondering how you go about modeling the group's physical atmosphere. Actually, there are a few things you *can* do. For instance, when the group members are present, you can arrange the furniture in a manner advantageous for discussion or some other group activity. Try asking the members if the temperature is comfortable and then make any needed adjustments. How about where you sit? Offer the best chair to someone else rather than always taking it because you usually arrive early. Perhaps among the best ideas is to model consideration by helping the host/hostess clean and straighten up after the meeting adjourns.

As you can see, creating the desired group climate involves planning and modeling all four atmosphere components. Please don't be overwhelmed by all this. It isn't as difficult as it may seem. In fact, just knowing about all these different issues is an excellent first step toward having great meetings. Be patient. Time and experience will increase your skills.

SETTING THE GROUP'S PACE

You, as the group leader, set the group's pace. Pace is on the opposite side of the coin from atmosphere. They are separate but related issues. If you recall in chapter four (see page 59) I defined "pace" as how quickly a group meeting moves and the tempo at which group activities are accomplished. Now in this section I want to look at another pace issue: modeling the desired group pace.

It's one thing to plan the meeting's activities and the desired pacing of the agenda, but making it happen is where your modeling comes in. It makes the critical difference between success and failure. Your attitudes and actions are far more influential in setting the group's pace than any other factors. This influence is especially true early in the group's existence when the members are still "checking out" one another and the group as a whole. Someone must establish the momentum to *get the group going and growing.* You as the leader are that person.

Four "D's" come to mind when I think about a group leader's role in modeling or setting the group's pace—degree, direction, distance, and divergence. Each "D" represents a different aspect or element of pacing. Working together, the four elements give us a fairly solid grip on what's involved in setting an effective pace. As you read the four descriptions, keep in mind that the individual elements don't exist by themselves. I've divided them up for explanation purposes. In reality they are four inter-dependent aspects of the same thing—pace.

Degree
The rate, speed, or quickness a group develops can vary. Too often this developmental issue is merely left to chance, and it just happens without any intentionality. In other words, it takes place "by default rather than by design" (this descriptive phrase also applies to many other group planning issues). How quickly should a group go in pursuing its purpose and goals? Again our standard answer when dealing with small groups is appropriate: *It all depends.* Finding an appropriate pace very much depends on the group and its goals. Yet there is one standard we can apply: *A measured pace is best.*

By "measured" I'm referring to a controlled or purposeful pace. It's important for you to demonstrate a desire to find a "right" pace—a speed the group members feel is appropriate. Behavior on your part that attempts to rush the group is as much to be avoided as just sitting back and letting things proceed as they may.

Degree can fluctuate. Moving swiftly may be appropriate at first, but at some point slowing down to "smell the roses" can also be beneficial. You need to model a willingness to fluctuate your leadership to comply with any needed changes in pace. Knowing when this is required comes from reading the group's atmosphere and talking with individual group members. Moving quickly in task groups may be desirable, while a slower, more measured pace often better fits need-based groups. Relational groups are difficult to discern because they can proceed at various rates at different times in their existence.

Direction

Moving rapidly or slowly without direction is wasted time and energy. Your example helps establish the group's *actual* direction. The group's purpose and goals may exist only on paper unless your attitudes and actions put "feet" on these guideposts.

Content or task groups are easier when it comes to modeling a correct direction. Since these kinds of groups' purpose and goals are less abstract, they lend themselves more quickly to establishing an appropriate pace or clear direction. Group members can more easily comprehend what is suitable leadership behavior in leading, for example, a Bible study. As a result, your modeling pays swifter dividends. On the other hand, relational and need-based groups frequently seek abstract, less definable goals. Consequently, it takes more effort and discernment to model a correct direction. Nevertheless, far more about the purpose and functioning of these kinds of groups is communicated through your modeling. Moreover, attitudes and behaviors you demonstrate during the early meetings set the pace for how the group functions thereafter.

Distance

Going in a determined direction and at an acceptable rate is important, but how far do you intend to go? "Distance" is the term that describes this factor associated with pace. How much do you want to accomplish and at what points in the journey? Once again, your example plays a vital role in answering these questions.

In task groups, your work habits and how much you accomplish set the pace. Rarely does a group finish its task in one meeting. Yet how much is accomplished in any given meeting is most often up to you—the pace you set. How far you go in a need-based group meeting, such as a support group, also depends on what you do. If you keep "pushing" the group, either they will proceed to where you're pushing or they will rebel and let you know you're shoving too hard. Applied to content groups, the issue is how much content to cover in one or a series of group meetings. If you set a fast pace, the group will attempt to cover as much as possible, to "travel an established distance." On the other hand, you can model a more leisurely pace and stop wherever the group is at when the meeting time runs out. In any case, avoid extremes . . . going too far or not far enough.

Divergence

The last pace issue I want to deal with is divergence—when to deviate from the pursued degree, direction, and distance. Divergence is more than planning variety in the meeting's agenda. The issue now is a wider focus. I'm talking about flexibility, an openness to consider deviating from the established plan and going at an appropriate pace when "people issues" arise. Modeling flexibility when such circumstances occur demonstrates to the group members you care more about them than you do about the group's planned agenda or program. Your group exists for the people, not the agenda you planned. It's always appropriate to diverge or change pace if it means better serving your members.

If this divergence process sounds similar to the discussion we had on spontaneity in chapter five, it should. We are just looking at a different aspect. In chapter five we focused on spontaneity within group meetings. Our present focus is on the whole group as it is functioning not only during but also beyond the regular meetings. It includes everything the group is and does, as well as your role in modeling and setting the group's pace. Divergence can be an important element in establishing and monitoring the group's overall pace.

Knowing when to deviate is the real challenge. I have no quick or simple advice to offer. My best suggestion is to listen to your members and the Holy Spirit. In your opinion you may be cruising along just fine when unexpectedly several members suggest a completely different pace for the group, which includes new goals, purpose, and so on. Talk and pray the suggestion through. Allow the group to decide for itself. Your role is to model a willingness to follow the Spirit's lead and do whatever is necessary to help the group succeed as a group.

SHARING LEADERSHIP

Perhaps among the most important modeling functions you must undertake is accepting and demonstrating shared leadership. There's no getting around it. What you model or *do* as a leader far outweighs what you *say* about leadership. Therefore, my goal in this chapter isn't to list and talk about all the various leadership functions—that is, what a leader does. Other authors, including myself, do that elsewhere. My purpose is to spend time examining the link between modeling and shared leadership.

Another "modeling verse" is helpful to begin our thinking about the relationship between shared leadership and modeling. Paul raised an interesting perspective worth noting. In fact, he added a new wrinkle when he talked about the Thessalonian believers imitating him. He said they "became imitators of *us*" (1 Thessalonians 1:6, NASB, emphasis added). Paul included Silvanus and Timothy as fellow leaders deserving imitation and recognized the Thessalonians for following them. He acknowledged both shared leadership and modeling in the same breath . . . an important principal! In my thinking, that attitude is vital to having great group meetings.

At the heart of shared leadership is delegation. You demonstrate acceptance and confidence in your group members when you entrust them with leadership responsibilities. Delegated tasks may be small at first and increase in size as the members become comfortable with one another and as you get to know which members are open to shared leadership. It may even mean accepting a person(s) to serve as your coleader(s), which leads us to the next subject.

You can model and facilitate shared leadership on several levels. The lowest level is to ask willing members to lead one specific activity during a group meeting. Next is having them lead an entire meeting in which they accept the responsibility to plan and conduct a meeting from start to finish. A third level involves serving as a coleader with you. A final level is reached when a member in your group accepts the responsibility to lead another separate group. Of course, these four levels don't have to proceed in the order in which they are described here. Furthermore, the attitudes and actions you model facilitate any or all of these steps. If you demonstrate your support for shared leadership, all four levels are possible.

Shared leadership also provides a context for you to model leadership roles and responsibilities for new and/or potential small group leaders. Some churches use a training program in which apprentice leaders work under a master leader, who explains and demonstrates what it takes to lead a successful small group. This method provides a real live context and a leader for the trainee to imitate. Once the apprenticeship is completed, the trainee starts or assumes leadership in another group.

More important than its functional benefits, shared leadership models a properly functioning body of Christ (see 1 Corinthians 12 and Ephesians 4). I cannot overemphasize this conceptual advantage. We talk about how the whole body is needed and must function together. While this knowledge is proper, *seeing* the body function together via shared leadership and your group in general is a dramatic picture not soon forgotten.

Finally, I contend that shared leadership increases the potential for planning and conducting great meetings. The old adage is true: Two (three, four, and more) heads are better than one.

TAKING ACTION

1. Thinking about what we can learn from the apostle Paul's example, what one or two points ring most true in your thinking?

2. How good are you at reading your group's "weather" (climate)? How can you improve?

3. Describe your group's atmosphere. How do you know your description is correct?

4. Describe your group's pace. As the leader, how do you influence your group's pace?

5. Explain how shared leadership works if it is used in your group.

CHAPTER SEVEN

Conducting Great Meetings: Doing It!

The time has come. You've planned and made all the necessary arrangements. Let the meeting begin. Well, not just yet. Let's pause for a moment to make certain everything is in fact ready to go.

CHECKING ONE LAST TIME

It never hurts to check one more time. Attention to small details makes for a huge success. After all, great meetings don't just happen. They are the product of good planning and scrupulous preparation.

Premeeting Review Process

Just prior to the group meeting—perhaps during the afternoon on the day the group meets in the evening—it's always wise to double check yourself to make certain you're actually ready. Go through a mental checklist, making sure everything is in order and prepared. Some leaders prefer to use a written checklist like the one on the next page (which can also serve as your mental checklist):

The suggested checklist, or one you devise, is merely a tool. You may find that it is quite helpful, especially when you first start leading a group. Over time you may discover you're using it less and less as your skill and confidence build. Don't feel guilty if this happens. That you are going through the premeeting review process is more important than the method you use to accomplish it. However you do it, just do it!

PREMEETING CHECKLIST

❏ I have committed the meeting to God in prayer and asked for His wisdom.

❏ I have reviewed the content and understand the main points.

❏ I have identified one or more objectives to guide the meeting.

❏ I have a potentially workable meeting agenda (activities, methods, times).

❏ I have prepared any needed handouts or other materials.

❏ I have all the supplies and/or equipment I need.

❏ I have made all necessary arrangements (setting, people, and so on).

❏ I have contacted the other members who have a part in the meeting (if there are any), and they are ready.

❏ I have a plan for determining how the meeting went (evaluation).

❏ I have confidence I can lead a great meeting with God's help.

Ready, Set, Go!

You're well prepared. Everything is set. Now let the meeting begin. Stop—not just yet. There's just one more task to do prior to actually conducting the meeting.

Plan to arrive early at wherever your group meets, even if the meeting is in your home. How early is up to you. Just be sure to budget enough time so you can complete any needed setup without being rushed. Ideally, by the time the first group member arrives, the setting is prepared, everything is ready, and you're primed to begin. There is something distinctive about entering a "cocked," well-prepared room—lights on, chairs arranged, handouts at each place, and visuals posted. The room itself tells the members "something is going to happen here tonight!" It's an important principal: A prepared environmental atmosphere heightens anticipation.

In addition to arriving early to make sure the setting is prepared, an early arrival provides two more valuable benefits. First, if you discover you forgot something or need to complete an unanticipated task, you have time to do whatever needs to be done before the meeting commences. This extra time or "safety buffer" can prevent ulcers (at least in hyper people like myself).

Second, and extremely important to me, an early arrival provides the opportunity for you to welcome the group members as they arrive. It's a small thing, but greeting the members at the door and offering a hearty welcome goes a long way in establishing relationships, setting the atmosphere, and promoting group cohesion (see page 54 in *How to Lead Small Groups*).

Now, go! Since all the preliminaries are accomplished, it's time to start the meeting . . . really! Pay close attention, because the remainder of this chapter deals with various meeting dynamics.

GETTING STARTED AND FINISHING ON TIME

A good start is always important, and among the most indispensable actions you can take to begin the meeting is to start on time. This seems quite obvious. Yet starting on time is actually among your more difficult tasks. There is always some reason to postpone starting—someone hasn't arrived yet, two members are talking in the kitchen, a member just arrived and is getting a cup of coffee, the telephone rings, or a whole host of other potential detractors are lurking about. It's far too easy to wait a minute or two. Don't! Start on time.

Why is starting on time so critical? First, because you are accountable as a time steward. That's right! Time is a stewardship. You are responsible—ultimately to God—for your and the other group members' time. As such, you don't want to waste it. People frequently drop out of groups when they think they're wasting time. Second, not beginning on time communicates to the members who do arrive and are ready to start on time that doing so isn't important. Soon they also begin arriving a little later each time. "Why not? We never start on time anyway." Before you know it, a meeting scheduled to start at 7 P.M. routinely starts at 7:15 P.M.

or later. Third, if starting on time was included in your group covenant, doing so demonstrates you take the covenant seriously. There is no use in having a covenant if it is ignored.

I'll say it again—start on time! If a group member protests, it's an opportunity to explain why you stress beginning on time. Kindly point out the agreed starting time was _____ (you fill in the blank), and it's your responsibility to follow the group's decision (covenant). It is *your* stewardship of *their* time. It seems there is always someone who is late to the meeting for whatever reason. Waiting for every member to show up before you start is futile. Besides, starting on time encourages everyone to arrive on time.

Last, starting on time allows the group to finish on time, which is equally important. I routinely conclude my meetings at the agreed upon time. On occasion this can be awkward because the meeting isn't at a logical stopping point. I handle this by announcing it's time to quit and then asking the group if they want to continue. If the group decides to keep going (be sure to decide on a specific amount of time), I point out it's acceptable to leave for those who must go. This latter move is important, because some members may need to pick up children, "rescue" the baby-sitter, attend to other business, get up early the next morning, and so on. It's unfair to group members not to finish on time or to make it difficult for them to leave when they must. In fact, if you habitually fail to end on time, don't be surprised if one or more members drop out.

Just because you end on time doesn't mean the members must leave. Depending on how the host or hostess feels, usually the group members are free to stay and talk as long as they want. I've been in several groups where the people enjoyed one another's company so much that they routinely stayed several hours after the meeting officially ended. In one case, we actually had to deal with the "problem" and decide on mutually agreeable time limits. This is the kind of problem I love.

To sum up this section, *be a clock watcher!* Nevertheless, I am *not* promoting overly compulsive behavior, following the clock to a point where it drives everyone crazy. What I am saying is that it's your responsibility as the leader to quietly monitor the clock to insure the group meetings begin and end on time. We live in a time-oriented society. Of course, not all cultures are as time conscious as we Americans are, but in most cases great meetings start and stop on time.

STAYING ON TRACK

In between starting and stopping on time, it's your privilege to lead the group's meeting. The desired goal, of course, is to have great meetings. This requires staying on track—that is, following your plan, staying focused, tracking your time, and practicing functional behaviors.

Use Your Plan

You wisely invested time and energy in planning the meeting. Now follow your plan. Stay flexible, but since you have a "destination" in mind, you need to keep moving in the right direction. Your plan is your road map. Two further suggestions: First, you may find it best to put your plan on 3 × 5 cards, and avoid making a big spectacle when you refer to your notes. Second, as you open the meeting, build anticipation among the members by quickly reviewing the agenda and, perhaps, sharing your objectives.

Stay Focused on Your Job

The biggest risk in leading group meetings is to become distracted by the content, engrossed in the discussion, or focused on the task, and then neglect your group leadership duties. Before you know it, the group is off track and wandering down some "bunny trail." Of course, staying tuned in is easier said than done. If you're like me, a verbal person with strongly held opinions, you'll struggle at first trying to find the right balance between your role as the leader and functioning as a group member. Some leaders go off the deep end and focus so intently on their leadership tasks that they mechanically lead the group without ever becoming a genuine group member.

Staying focused on your leadership role is especially important during the group's early development. However, as the group "matures" and formal and informal shared leadership begins to take hold, the group members themselves are more likely to engage in functional behaviors (which is discussed on the next page) that help the group stay on track. As this dynamic takes hold, you become more free to participate as a "regular" group member. Even so, don't forget that you're still the leader and may have to perform as such at any time.

Again, Be a Clock Watcher

Warning: this time issue needs to be stressed again! Time management is among your primary duties and requires your continued focus if you are to succeed in helping the group stay on track during its meetings. No one is suggesting you rigidly follow the specific times you planned for each agenda item. By all means, some flexibility is essential. You must remain sensitive to the Holy Spirit's direction. My point is that you help the group proceed in an unobtrusive, orderly manner. It's too easy to get off track and waste valuable time on silly discussions or other questionable activities. To avoid this danger, keep your eye on the clock and gently coax the group along. At times, however, you may need to overtly call their attention to the time and ask for their cooperation to move on, or you may need to lead the group in deciding to abandon the plan and follow the Spirit's leading.

Functional Behaviors

Certain functional or practical behaviors help group meetings stay on track and are necessary for you to practice as the group leader. Many books on small groups include items similar to the following list:

◆ Gate keeping—Enabling all members to participate in discussions and suggesting limits on participation so everyone has a chance to contribute.

◆ Encouraging—Friendly words and actions that praise, are supportive, demonstrate personal warmth and responsiveness to others, and recognize contributions.

◆ Reflecting—Feedback that summarizes apparent group feelings and describe group reactions to ideas or suggestions.

◆ Listening—Hearing what group members have to say about the content or group processes and responding in an appropriate fashion.

◆ Clarifying—Explaining group processes or procedures and asking for opinions to establish facts.

◆ Standard setting—Reminding members about group norms.

◆ Consensus testing—Asking for opinions in order to tentatively find out if the group is nearing consensus on a decision and tossing around ideas to test group opinions.

◆ Following—Accepting group decisions, allowing the group to function without direct intervention, and using others' ideas.

◆ Harmonizing—Mediating and reconciling differences among members and suggesting possible compromise solutions.

◆ Tension reducing—Easing negative situations and/or member feelings by speaking calmly or by light jesting, while putting things into context and perspective.

Ultimately the functional behaviors listed above are the whole group's responsibility. You as the leader need to explain and model these essential interpersonal behaviors during the group's early meetings. Why? Because great meetings that foster cooperation, mutual support, interdependence, and member satisfaction are more likely when group members individually and corporately share the responsibility for the group's successful functioning with you.

HELPING MEMBERS PARTICIPATE

Great meetings are great because the members are involved and enjoy their involvement. To make this happen, the following suggestions are some productive things you can do to help the members participate effectively in the group meetings.

Clear Questions and Instructions

I don't know how many times I've been in a group in which the leader asked a long, complicated question or gave vague instructions for the next activity. In response, the members just sat there staring at one another not knowing how to answer or what to do. Sound familiar? Avoid repeating this scene by preparing your questions beforehand (see page 91 in *How to Lead Small Groups*) and making certain your activity instructions are clear and logical. When it comes to group activities, try doing whatever it is you intend to ask the group to do prior to the meeting so you can get a "feel" for the activity. You'll be amazed how much better your instructions are if you speak from firsthand experience.

At times you'll need to "wing it" and ask unplanned questions or make up instructions on the spot for an unplanned method. Don't worry about it. However, if you're new to leading a small group and you expect to operate in this fashion *on a regular basis*, I warn you that you're in for a rough time. It's far better to prepare and deviate from your plan than it is to lead a group without proper preparation and hope everything works out. The latter strategy is poor stewardship in my opinion.

Ask in Advance

For the first three or four months (an approximate guess since your group may differ), I recommend you avoid surprising members by asking them to do something during the group meeting (such as pray, read, or respond). You're always safe if *prior* to the meeting, you ask the person whether he or she is willing to do whatever it is you want done. Don't twist arms or lay on a heavy load of guilt. Members need to feel free to say no as quickly as you want them to say yes. Of course, *how* you ask is also important. A demanding tone rarely results in a positive response. Ask people to do things you're willing to do and in a manner you would appreciate if they were asking you. It's simple common courtesy.

Several groups I've been in didn't need to observe this "ask in advance" guideline. Everyone knew one another fairly well and weren't rattled when the leader spontaneously asked them to do something during the meetings. In general, the better the group members know one another, the less advance notice you need to give.

Don't Force Members to Talk

Some authors suggest methods to get everyone to verbally participate in group meetings. I don't. Not everyone is as verbal as the next person. Some people are quiet by nature. Consequently, forcing members to verbally participate isn't always a good idea. For example, my wife is a highly intelligent woman with many good ideas. Yet by personality she is a quiet person. She rarely talks during group meetings. But when she does, you can bank on what she says. Forcing her to talk isn't necessary (and would get me into trouble if I did).

While not wanting to force people to talk, you do want to initiate an atmosphere that encourages the members' participation if and when they feel comfortable doing so. This ideal climate is something you establish beginning with the first meeting and maintain throughout the group's entire life. The functional behaviors we previously reviewed play a significant role in creating this desired participation atmosphere.

Deal with "Personalities" Outside Group Meetings

You and other group members can easily deal with many necessary "adjustments" in other members' attitudes and behavior patterns in non-combative ways during the group meetings. Your effective modeling can accomplish much. The situation may arise, however, when you do all the right things and the other members are being patient, but a member is definitely "stepping over the line," and something must be done. If this occurs, my recommendation is to deal with the situation outside the group meeting. Make an appointment to have coffee or lunch, or to meet during some other casual activity. Express your appreciation for the individual and his or her group membership (at least find something positive to say). Kindly point out the offending behavior and ask what you can do to help him or her deal with the challenge. After exploring the situation and determining an acceptable course of action, be sure to conclude with prayer and thank the person for his or her cooperation. Lord willing, your dilemma will be solved, but don't be surprised if it doesn't work out that easily.

Usually group members quickly receive corrective action *if* you approach them in a kind and considerate manner. Few people want to cause problems. Nevertheless, some people (hopefully not in your group) have a personality that seems to enjoy conflict or who have serious personal problems, preventing "normal" group participation. If your attempt at dealing with these personalities outside the group meeting fails, move quickly to get help from your pastor or other qualified individuals. The group's well-being, and your own, is at stake. Most groups and group leaders are not equipped to deal with people who evidence psychological/emotional instability.

In the final analysis, sometimes you must ask a person to step out of the group until the complicating personal situation is resolved. Don't feel badly about this, but please don't abandon the person either. Make any necessary arrangements to help the person overcome the circumstances and/or find another suitable group, such as a need-based group.

Be Patient

My best advice when it comes to helping members participate is simply to *be patient* with them and yourself. New group leaders frequently expect too much too soon. As I've already said, every group is different and progresses at its own rate. Yes, you can help speed things along, but pushing and shoving isn't wise. On the positive side, have the group discuss their comfort level with various potential group activities and methods. You might be surprised by how much the members are ready to "move."

You may find the following participation model useful, for it is designed to help group members systematically move from nonparticipation to active group-leadership participation. As with all models, please keep in mind that it is a generalization.

PARTICIPATION MODEL

How do I help my group members become active participants? Unfortunately, there are no easy answers. No single method or strategy works every time. Nevertheless, the following "model" presents four steps you can take in helping your group members become active participants. Be sure to review the "issues" section, which further explains the model, after you review the model itself. Note: It's okay to adjust the model to suit your group's personality and needs.

STEP ONE: Individual Involvement
Ask members to participate just as individuals, by themselves. Select methods which require no interaction with other group members (for example, silent prayer, reading worksheet, and so forth).

Goal: To build the members' general "comfort level" with activity-oriented participation.

STEP TWO: One-on-One Involvement
Ask the members to work/interact with one other group member; the same person or different people week to week; limited interaction with other group members. Two "sharing levels" are possible (see "issues"): (A) impersonal and (B) personal.

Goal: To assist the group members in becoming comfortable interacting on a limited basis with another group member.

STEP THREE: Sub-Group Involvement
Ask the members to form sub-groups consisting of 3, 4, 6 people, men, women, and so forth. Interaction is now extended to more than one individual at a time. Again, two sharing levels are possible: (A) impersonal and (B) personal.

(Continued on page 107)

(Continued from page 106)

Goal: Building upon their comfort level interacting with one person, to increase participation to include additional group members at the same time.

STEP FOUR: Whole Group Involvement

Ask group members to do something for the whole group (for example, pray or read out loud, share a comment, and so forth); some members advance to leading group activities or the entire group meeting; maximum interpersonal interaction. As in the two previous steps, two sharing levels are possible: (A) impersonal and (B) personal.

Goal: To facilitate maximum participation and interaction in keeping with the group's purpose and membership.

Issues Affecting the Group Participation Model

1. *Your Group*: Every group is different. Some groups skip Step One altogether and move rapidly to Step Four. Other groups—often content or task group—must start at the first step and progress slowly, perhaps never reaching Step Four. While the steps are presented in a logical order, frequently groups "skip around" and don't follow the model exactly as depicted. Furthermore, once the members feel comfortable (if ever) operating at all four levels, then you may use one or more levels within the same group meeting.

2. *Your Individual Members*: Expect diversity among your group members. Often members vary in their ability to operate at the various steps. Some members feel totally comfortable functioning at Step Four, others do not. Don't be surprised if your group members demonstrate impatience with fellow members who cannot function at the higher steps. Keep in mind, some people simply don't feel comfortable sharing personal information or taking leadership roles before the whole group.

3. *Time*: There is no set, required time it takes to move from step to step. You have to "feel" your way along. One group may move rapidly, while the next may never get beyond Step Two or Step Three. Group members' backgrounds and the group's purpose

(Continued on page 108)

(Continued from page 107)

affect the time required at each step. Many groups limit their meetings to interaction at steps one and two in the beginning. Only after the group has met for months and the members feel comfortable with each other are they able to advance to steps three and four. The best way to determine how fast to move is to discuss the matter with the group members.

4. *Interaction*: Interpersonal interaction is a key dimension within small groups and takes place in many ways. But for our purposes, I am referring to verbal interaction. Each step in the participation model elevates the amount of verbal interaction in which members participate. Step One has none. Step Four requires the most interaction.

5. *Sharing Levels*: Interaction between group members is characterized by sharing at two levels: impersonal or personal. Normally starting with impersonal, members merely share facts and information, nothing more than "name, rank, and serial number." Personal feelings, opinions, and experiences aren't included. Only at the second level, the personal sharing level, do members begin to express more intimate information about their personal backgrounds, opinions, hopes, fears, etc. As expected, determining when to move from impersonal sharing to more personal levels depends on the specific group's purpose and members. Some groups are not intended to facilitate or choose not to facilitate deeply personal interaction among the members. Ideally, most groups seek to establish a healthy sharing level which falls some where in between the two possible extremes depicted in the illustration below (your group's ideal sharing level may not fall in the exact middle as shown).

Impersonal
No personal
information

Ideal
Sharing
Level

Personal
All personal
information

FLEXING TO MEET NEEDS

We already discussed spontaneity in chapter five. It is while the meeting is in progress that spontaneity potentially comes into play. Many things, however, can generate spontaneity, which may or may not be related to meeting needs. In my thinking, flexing to meet a group member's need during a meeting fits into spontaneity's "special case" category. It is a special kind of focused, spontaneous action.

For example, I recall a member in a previous group who was experiencing tremendous personal struggles brought on by a divorce she was going through. At one meeting she broke down and began to cry. The other group members quickly discerned the need to set aside my planned meeting. The evening was spent talking and praying with this hurting individual. Flexing to meet her needs was a good thing. Everyone felt happy about what we did.

Needs aren't always spiritual or emotional in nature. Your group may find itself needing to flex and end the meeting early because the home in which you meet doesn't have electricity due to a storm (this actually happened to me once). Other similar administrative, organizational, or facility issues may create "needs" that demand your flexibility.

On the "people" side, should you flex to meet every need expressed by a group member? It's hard to say. There are no clear-cut answers. Whether it's an administrative or people need, I suggest that group flexibility may be warranted in the following situations:

◆ When the expressed need is something the group can deal with at the present time
◆ When the member expressing the need asks for help then and there
◆ When the situation prevents the meeting from continuing
◆ When no members strenuously object to any actions or decisions that affect the whole group and that are necessary to address the expressed need
◆ Your suggestions

Again, be a clock watcher! Flexing to meet needs is good, but doing so impacts the group's time agenda. You may find it necessary to cancel the meeting, extend the time, or pick up the meeting "midstream" after dealing with a situation that doesn't consume all the group's time. In any case, be prepared to adjust the agenda to fit the available time.

KNOWING WHEN TO QUIT

Good leaders not only know how to plan and lead meetings, but also know how to end meetings. Interestingly enough, there are two dimensions to knowing when to quit: (1) ending a meeting and, ultimately, (2) ending the group. We'll consider each dimension.

Ending the Meeting

The obvious answer to when to quit is when the time is up. In most cases this works. On occasion, however, it isn't that simple. Take the example I mentioned in the last section, the one in which the group member was going through a divorce. Telling the members to stop because the time was up while they were deeply engaged in dealing with this woman's tense, emotional situation would have demonstrated heartless insensitivity, as you can well imagine. A better approach was to either say nothing and allow individual members to decide when they must leave or to quietly dismiss the group and invite those who can stay to do so.

Ending a meeting is not, of course, always traumatic. In most cases it's rather routine. Even so, be sure to do the following before officially adjourning:

◆ Thank the members for participating.
◆ Review any assignments or activities that need completion prior to the next meeting.
◆ If the group has shared leadership, indicate who is responsible for the next meeting.
◆ Remind them about any group or church activities coming up on the calendar.
◆ If necessary, make certain they know when and where the next meeting will be held.
◆ Close with prayer.

One last time, be a (reasonable, sane) clock watcher! Remember, you are a time steward and quitting on time is as important as starting on time.

Ending the Group

It's not unusual for groups to keep trying to become an effective group when in truth it's best for them to recognize it isn't going to work and "pull the plug." No one wants to think they've failed. Nevertheless, honesty is still the best policy. It does the group, you, or your members no good to fool yourselves into thinking the group is going to become something it's not. Ending the group doesn't always mean failure; sometimes it's the best option.

I recommend you consider ending your group when one or more of these conditions exist (ideally it's a total group decision):

◆ When at least half the members express interest in doing so
◆ When at least half the group members are routinely absent
◆ When the members just don't "click" together after repeated attempts
◆ When disharmony exists, and it cannot be resolved
◆ When the group completes its task (task-oriented groups)
◆ When it becomes clear to all the members the group isn't likely to achieve its purpose
◆ When whatever circumstances unique to your situation indicate it's the best alternative
◆ Your suggestions

KNOWING IF IT WAS A GREAT MEETING

The meeting is about to end or it's over. How do you know whether or not it was a great meeting? Other than your perceptive feelings, are there ways you can determine whether or not the meeting was a success? You bet there is! Other than formal evaluation, which I discuss in both *How to Lead Small Groups* and *How to Build a Small Groups Ministry*, there are several informal methods you can use. First, try asking the members the simple question, "How did it go tonight (this afternoon, this morning)?" Mature groups—ones with members who enjoy high mutual trust and appreciation—are able to provide honest, immediate feedback. An informal five-minute conversation can yield extremely useful information on what went well and what didn't.

Second, try a quick rating system. This option works better in groups who haven't been together long and whose trust level is still building.

Pass out 3 × 5 cards and ask the members to write three things: (1) a number between 1 (low) and 10 (high) that represents their overall rating for that particular meeting; (2) something they did at this meeting they would like to do again at future meetings; and (3) anything that made them uncomfortable or was boring. Prior to passing out the cards, explain that you need feedback so you can plan and lead great meetings for them. You may also want to tell them not to put their names on their cards. Use your judgment. You know your group members better than I.

A third option is to briefly chat with several members prior to their leaving or to call them on the telephone during the ensuing week. Key to this method is selecting individuals you think will share their honest opinions. Some group members may not wish to tell you what they really think. If they actually don't like what's happening, they usually "vote with their feet" and find an excuse for not coming back.

Don't put undue pressure on yourself. Every group meeting cannot be a winner. Nevertheless, many group leaders avoid seeking *any* feedback for fear they aren't doing a good job or because they simply don't want to change. I feel sorry for these leaders because they are missing the point. Conversely, if you or the group members identify something needing change, be swift to make the necessary corrections (see Proverbs 13:10).

The more group meetings you lead, the better you'll become at it. Conducting great meetings is a skill almost everyone can learn. When those less than perfect meetings occur, and you'll have your share, accept them as your opportunity for the Holy Spirit to teach you something. Just keep going. And remember: God is the real group leader; you're just the assistant leader!

TAKING ACTION

1. Describe what you do (premeeting checklist) to insure you are ready to conduct a great group meeting.

2. Does your group start and finish on time? If not, what can you do to comply with this important expectation?

3. As you review the "functional behaviors" (pp. 102-103), identify two that are your strengths and two you need to work on. What can you do to strengthen the two that need work?

4. Review the suggestions in the "Helping Members Participate," then add any additional suggestions you may have. Which suggestions do you think will work in your group?

5. Describe where your group is on the "Participation Model" (see pages 106-108). What can you do to increase your group's participation level?

6. What do you plan to do at your next meeting to determine whether or not it will be a great meeting?

CHAPTER EIGHT

Insights: Potentially Great Meetings and Ideas

The final chapter. Congratulations on coming this far. Now I invite you to turn your attention to some potential great meeting suggestions and several good ideas associated with having great meetings.

The following suggestions represent proven small group meeting formats and ideas. As such, I recommend that you try them. Be sure, of course, to make any adjustments you think are necessary for the context and needs of your small group.

GETTING INVOLVED IN GROUP SERVICE PROJECTS

It's fairly easy for a group to lapse into a comfortable routine and become self-sufficient and self-serving. Before you know it, even without trying, the group can quickly function inwardly and develop an exclusive identity, which others outside the group describe as a "clique." As you know, a self-centered group whose members think only of themselves may unintentionally, yet routinely, exclude others from their group. Rarely does a group plan on this happening. It just does. Why? Most often it's because the group has no external activity or emphasis. All their time and energy is spent on the group itself. This is especially true for groups with fixed memberships and who focus on relationships or content, but it can happen to any group.

One viable method to help the group avoid becoming a self-centered clique is to encourage the group to participate in service projects—that is, specific actions designed to serve others for a specified time. Some groups focus totally on service projects; it's the reason they exist. In chapter one we classified such groups as "task groups." Yet every group, regardless of type, needs to consider engaging in some kind of service. Groups need to find ways to serve others outside their group.

Finding service opportunities for the group requires some creativity on your part. Talk with your pastor, check with local social service agencies, ask other group leaders, brainstorm with your group members, or talk with a deacon or an elder. The opportunities are numerous. You just have to keep your eyes and ears open. Some alternatives are suitable for one-time projects; others may require your group to commit to multiple sessions. Moreover, be sure everyone in your group participates in selecting the project. Attempting to force the members to do something they don't want to do isn't in the group's best interests.

Here are some potential group service project ideas you may want to consider using (at the end of the list are a few blank checks for you to add your own ideas):

✓ Serve meals at the local rescue mission.
✓ Adopt a widow in your church (James 1:27).
✓ Volunteer at a pro-life counseling center.
✓ Be bell ringers for the Salvation Army during the Christmas season.
✓ Identify a community-based organization you can assist.
✓ Serve your church by being ushers once per month.
✓ Volunteer to run the nursery on a regular basis.
✓ Provide baby-sitting for other groups.
✓ Be big brothers and big sisters.
✓ Take a missions trip to a foreign country.
✓ Spend a Saturday cleaning your church.
✓ Help the pastor with hospital visitation.
✓
✓
✓

How often does a group participate in service projects? Fortunately, there isn't a fixed answer. Each group must decide for itself. Some groups do it on an unscheduled basis, whenever the opportunity arises. Other groups prefer to be involved in service projects on a regularly scheduled basis. For example, a recent group I was in decided to have a "rotating format." As a relationship-oriented group, we scheduled our four monthly meetings to include two sermon discussions, one prayer meeting (we prayed every meeting, but we dedicated one entire meeting per month to learning about and practicing prayer), and a service project. By the way, in the months with five meeting dates, we dedicated the fifth meeting to a family-oriented event. We had a game night, went on a picnic, watched a video, or did something else that was fun.

In the example I just described, doing a service project became a regular meeting option. Other groups maintain their regular meeting format, but add service projects from time to time. There is no one way it must be done. Do whatever best fits your group's purpose and objectives.

PLAYING TOGETHER

No matter what type of group I've been in, I've found it profitable for the members to participate in recreational activities together. In fact, playing together provides the following benefits:

◆ Builds relationships among group members
◆ Helps members know each other as people, who have both strengths and weaknesses
◆ Provides a break in the group's routine
◆ Keeps the group "fresh" and dynamic
◆ Provides the opportunity to include the members' entire families

I don't offer any potential recreational activities for your group to consider because the possibilities are far too numerous to list. Your group can come up with many alternatives on its own. We all have our favorite recreational activities. Moreover, the many regional and seasonal alternatives would fill this book. Therefore, sit down with your group members and put together your own list. Playing together can result in some great meetings.

May I offer a cautionary note, however? Avoid losing sight of your group's purpose and objectives. I've seen many groups drift off center because their recreational activities began to consume their time together. What was a good idea to stimulate relationships among the members became the group's dominant motivation. Conversely, one strategy for group development is to begin with a social agenda, and after the group members know each other, move on to "deeper" things. This strategy can work, but I haven't seen it often succeed.

MEETING WITH OTHER GROUPS

Broaden your group's social and spiritual horizons by occasionally meeting with another group or groups. Whether this means one meeting or a series of meetings, the interaction with other groups nurtures the individual groups, the groups ministry, and your total church body. Interaction between groups also helps the groups avoid becoming isolated and overly introspective.

In my opinion, groups are mainly for adults, and they function best when the adult members are fairly close in age (usually within ten year age spans). Nevertheless, isolating the various age groups from one another isn't healthy or even necessary. Thus one way to avoid age-group isolation is to have occasional joint meetings. For example, encourage a young-marrieds group to meet with a senior-citizens group. What about asking a single adults group to join a group of middle-aged married couples to complete a service project? The sky's the limit; the options and alternatives are endless.

Meetings with other groups may also include gatherings among different group types. For instance, your relational group may choose to invite a task group to join you for a social event. Another possibility might be a content group electing to meet with a need-based group to study a particular biblical theme both groups find interesting. Members in one type of group are helped when they see how a different kind of group functions; it expands their knowledge about groups and hopefully gives them an appreciation for the diversity existing within the body of Christ. In fact, the concept of groups meeting together is a valuable strategy even in smaller churches that only have one kind of group or where the groups are intergenerational (mixed ages).

When you decide to meet with another group, keep the following suggestions in mind:

◆ Plan the arrangements well in advance and be sure everyone knows the particulars.

◆ Be certain someone accepts the responsibility to plan and lead the combined meeting(s).

◆ Devote an appropriate amount of time introducing the group members to one another.

◆ Whatever the meeting format and agenda, be sure everyone understands.

◆ After the joint meeting, when your group meets separately again, invest a few minutes "debriefing" the experience. Should you do it again? Why or why not?

PLANNING AND ENJOYING SPECIAL OCCASIONS

Holidays, birthdays, community and church events all serve as opportunities for your group to plan and enjoy a special, great meeting. The idea of meetings revolving around special occasions is a fairly straightforward one that doesn't demand much explanation. Nevertheless, here are some guidelines for your consideration (once again, I left some checks for you to add your own suggestions):

✓ Select special occasions that are meaningful to all your group members.

✓ Many special occasion meetings are social in nature, but religious holidays present a great opportunity for the group to do a topical study on the holiday's significance (such as Easter and Christmas).

✓ Make up a holiday to celebrate. For example, "group day," celebrating the date your group first began to meet.

✓ Rather than celebrating every member's exact birthday, have a birthday party each quarter for everyone with a birthday during that period.

✓ As with any meeting, be sure someone is responsible to plan and lead the meeting.

✓ Don't overdo it; too many special occasion meetings dulls the concept.

✓

✓

✓

ORGANIZING PRAYER PARTNERS AND CHAINS

Among the especially good group ideas is having prayer partners and prayer chains. I'm convinced every group—no matter what its purpose—needs to include prayer as a vital element in its meetings. After all, what better activity can a group do together than to talk with God? I find it awesome that God wants us to communicate with Him both individually *and* corporately. Therefore, both prayer partners and chains deserve our careful consideration.

Prayer Partners

The basic idea is to divide the group members into pairs, each paired member pledging to pray with and for his or her partner. To illustrate, let's say a group has twelve members (six couples—six women and six men), and they decide to randomly pair the men with men and the women with women. They further decide to phone each other every other day, with each pair deciding on the best time. During the brief telephone conversation, the goal is to do three things: (1) "check in" with each other; (2) review old and share new prayer requests; and (3) pray. The group has decided to limit their telephone calls to ten or fifteen minutes.

The previous example is only one option. Feel free to tailor the concept to your group's needs and interests. In doing so, keep the following suggestions in mind:

❑ Prayer partners usually work best when the partners are the same gender.

❑ There is no required method for selecting partners. Allow the group members to decide how they want to pair up.

❑ There are no time limits on how long the partners remain partners; one week, one month, one year—all are acceptable. Consider rotating partners at least once per year.

❑ Prayer partners need to determine what format to use. Examples might include phoning each other in the morning, meeting for lunch on Tuesdays, or keeping a running e-mail prayer list. The options are limitless. Using more than one format or changing formats is also workable.

❑ Prayer partners normally involve two people. But given what you judge as the correct circumstances, there is no reason why there cannot be as many as four partners (the maximum number) in a prayer cell.

Prayer Chains

Prayer chains are common and work well in most churches. Likewise, the prayer chain idea functions well within groups. This makes sense. Small groups are nothing more than your church (or *the* church) in a different organizational form.

Most longtime church members are familiar with prayer chains. But to refresh our memories or to introduce the idea to younger believers, I will describe the "typical" group-oriented prayer chain. A group member has a personal prayer request or learns about someone who needs prayer. This member immediately calls the group's "prayer captain" (or whatever title works for you), who is responsible for calling designated group members. They in turn call the remaining group members until everyone receives the prayer request. In most cases no one calls more than two or three people to complete the prayer chain.

Groups can link together and form larger prayer chains as well. When a member has a prayer request, that person contacts the group's prayer captain, who (A) starts the prayer chain within her or his own group and (B) starts the chain in other groups by calling other predetermined group prayer captains, who in turn repeat steps A and B until the chain is completed. Thus even though the groups are separate, they are bound together in prayer. It's an effective method to communicate care and concern among the various groups. Likewise, it's an opportunity to pass on selected information.

Are there any downsides to these prayer methods? Not really. It's possible, of course, for them to degenerate into gossip chains, but with a little monitoring this potential malady can be avoided. It's also averted by selecting your group's prayer captain wisely and making certain he or she understands the following guidelines:

- ◆ The originating prayer captain is obligated to secure accurate facts and information before passing on any prayer request.
- ◆ Make every attempt to pass on prayer requests within one hour after they are received.
- ◆ When the party you are calling comes to the phone (1) identify yourself, (2) state it is a prayer chain call, (3) state the prayer

request, (4) thank the person for praying, and in some cases, (5) share whatever other significant information you need to relay, then (6) hang up.

◆ Avoid speculation. Refrain from "reading between the lines" or adding information you think is true but aren't certain about.

◆ If you think it is appropriate, pray with the person making the prayer request and with those individuals you contact to transmit the request.

◆ Limit any additional information passed on during the telephone call to items that are mutually beneficial. In other words, get to the point and hang up. Prayer chain calls must not become general conversations (at least in most cases).

Prayer partners and chains contribute to an underlying group dynamic that paves the way for having great meetings. We must realize great meetings require more than a well-planned and executed agenda. Strong interpersonal relationships among the group members are essential in facilitating great meetings, and, without a doubt, praying together encourages such relationships.

IMPLEMENTING OUTREACH

When I use the term "outreach," I'm describing two possible group activities: (1) evangelism, seeking to share the gospel with nonbelievers, and (2) assimilation, seeking to incorporate new believers or new visitors who are already Christians into your church via your small group. Some task groups focus on either or both evangelism and assimilation as their specific purpose for existing. Other types of groups elect to include various outreach methods as a regular group activity or perhaps as an occasional group project. Whether it is the primary focus or one activity added to their regular format, groups need to consider outreach meetings.

Evangelism

Banding together as a group to evangelize is a terrific idea. However, this is among the most difficult of group formats or activities I know. Most believers understand they should share the gospel, but feel awkward doing so. Besides, I'm not convinced every small group, as a group, must engage in evangelism. In my thinking some groups are designed for Christians alone. These groups are designed to stimulate Christian growth and fellowship, not to bring nonbelievers to Christ. Evangelism is vital to a church and in every Christian's life, but this does not mean it's a required activity for every group. Nonetheless, evangelism is an excellent group activity, and for groups who wish to participate, here are some guidelines to follow:

✓ Have a plan. You're wise to search out and use materials designed to assist your group in planning and conducting evangelism.
✓ Be sure everyone in the group is "onboard" and willing to participate.
✓ Keep in mind your responsibility is to share the good news. It's the Holy Spirit's task to convict and convince a person to receive Jesus Christ as his or her personal Savior.

Assimilation
Small groups are an outstanding method to assimilate new people into your church. Your group can serve as a people-to-people strategy for helping visitors get to know church members and feel comfortable in your congregation. To do this, you may want to keep your group's membership open—anyone can come at any time—or elect to plan specific meetings designed to invite new members. Either option is workable. Here are some assimilation tips for your consideration:

✓ Have a plan. How do people come? Were they invited to attend your group? What do you do when they show up?
✓ Tailor your meeting agenda, if necessary, to accommodate visitors, or devise a meeting format especially for the occasion.
✓ Have a strategy ready to follow up with visitors. Thank them for coming and invite them back.
✓ Be prepared for the "disruption" to group trust and cohesion resulting from "strangers" visiting your group.

Last, keep the following general ideas in mind as you think about your group's involvement with outreach—both evangelism and assimilation:

◆ Sadly, many Christians feel uncomfortable with outreach activities. Consequently, you're wise to discuss the concept with your group before undertaking any such meetings.

◆ Outreach changes the group's complexion; that is, the group changes every time a new member is added. Be prepared to invest time in helping new members become integrated into the group's identity and relationships.

◆ Don't expect everyone in your group to operate at the high level you desire. Many Christians might agree with evangelism and assimilation, but decline to participate when given the opportunity. In fact, they may be absent at that meeting, do just enough to get by, or drop out of the group altogether.

◆ Task groups that focus on either evangelism or assimilation, or both, work best doing these kinds of activities. Why? Because the group members know this is why they are a group and have already elected to participate.

◆ For other types of groups, make certain from the very beginning that the members understand evangelism and/or assimilation are included in the group's format or at least are possibilities. I've seen several groups fall apart after announcing they were responsible for evangelizing when they didn't know in advance this was an expectation.

◆ Always, always, always have a plan—a plan everyone understands and accepts.

SAYING "I'M SORRY"

Like people, on occasion a group must say, "I'm sorry." Circumstances demanding this action fall into two categories: (1) internal, the group offends or does something to anger a member; and (2) the group some-how offends someone outside the group (for example, another group leader or member, the pastor, an elder, a custodian, or the church board). Great meetings are impossible if you have people angry within the group or at your group.

Internal
Circumstances may warrant devoting an entire meeting to dealing with hurt feelings among the group members. I've seen many occasions where

group members did something to offend one of their fellow members. Usually it was unintentional. Nevertheless, it occurred. In response, the group needed to deal with the resulting interpersonal wounds.

Ignoring or discounting hurt feelings is risky. Left to fester, they can easily grow and cause worse problems. Therefore, it's always best to deal with "intragroup" difficulties as soon as possible. Saying "I'm sorry" is important and necessary. In doing so, you'll want to observe the following rules:

✓ Be honest and straightforward.

✓ Don't dwell on causes or seek to place blame in attempting to name and deal with the hurt or offense.

✓ Ask for forgiveness and determine what restitution, if any, is needed.

✓ Pray together.

External
While a rare event, there are times when a group does or says something that offends people outside the group. Should this occur, a special meeting may be required to deal with the situation. For instance, suppose your group plans an all-day outing and intends to use the church van. Without making prior arrangements, one of your group members picks up the van early Saturday morning and then returns it late that evening. To your horror you learn that another group had reserved the van for the day while still another group was scheduled to use it that evening. Naturally, these people are upset with you. Your group needs to apologize. After talking about it, your group decides to invite the "offended parties" to a special "I'm sorry dinner" in their honor. The invitations admit your transgression, ask for their forgiveness, and request their presence at the dinner. On the designated evening, be upbeat, but be honest. Thank them for their willingness to forgive your group (assuming they are), and pledge you'll never do it again (be sure to keep your word!).

Of course, given the situation just described, you could respond by doing nothing about it, but this option isn't recommended. Even if you said "I'm sorry" only in a letter or phone call and skipped the dinner (or some other option), you must acknowledge your error and deal with its effects. Failure to do so goes against the unity the apostle Paul encouraged us to maintain (see Ephesians 4:2-3).

SERVING ONE ANOTHER

Great meetings are possible when you and your group practice the principle Paul set forth in his letter to the Galatians, "Through love serve one another" (Galatians 5:13, NASB). During or outside your meetings, serving one another puts flesh on Jesus' commandment to "love one another" (John 13:34).

Serving one another is a group's opportunity to practice being the body of Christ. We talk about service, but the group context makes it possible to translate the talk into action. I get excited when I find a group who takes seriously this opportunity and challenge. Whatever the format or agenda, great meetings are common when the group members are committed to serving one another.

Many options are possible, but here are some workable ideas to serve one another (add your own suggestions to the list):

❑ Regard other members as more important than yourself (Philippians 2:3).
❑ Baby-sit for each other.
❑ Pray for one another (James 5:16).
❑ Take meals to the family when someone is sick.
❑ Don't lie to one another (Colossians 3:9).
❑ Send an encouraging note.
❑ Act with humility toward one another (1 Peter 5:5).
❑ Help one another with home projects.
❑ Don't complain about one another (James 5:9).
❑ Mow a member's lawn while that person is on vacation.
❑ Encourage one another (1 Thessalonians 5:11).
❑ Teach Sunday school.
❑
❑
❑

Note the representative "one another" verses I included in the above list; many others are possible. Your group is an outstanding framework in which to learn about and practice the many attitudes and actions Scripture says should exist among believers. Small groups are designed to serve one another.

Well, that wraps it up! You now have some workable ideas on how to help your group have really great meetings. But remember, great meetings don't just happen, they take planning, time, effort, and ample prayer. Go to it!!

TAKING ACTION

1. Identify two or three service projects to present to your group for adoption.

2. Describe how your group has fun together. Then determine whether or not those fun activities are in balance with your group's purpose and goals.

3. Are there other groups with whom your group can potentially meet? If there are, discuss it with your group and plan a joint meeting.

4. Does your group have prayer partners or a prayer chain? If not, are these ideas good for your group? If they are, how do you plan to introduce the ideas?

5. Explain how outreach fits into your group's purpose and goals.

6. List ways you can serve your group members and ways the group members can serve one another.

Endnotes

Chapter Two:
The Planning Process: Knowing Where You're Going

1. Carl F. George, *Prepare Your Church for the Future* (Old Tappan, NJ: Revell, 1991).
2. Based on Martha M. Leypoldt *Learning Is Change* (Valley Forge, PA: Judson Press, 1971).

Chapter Three:
Participation: Helping Everyone Become Involved

1. See "S13-Groups Covenant" in Neal F. McBride, *How to Build a Small Groups Ministry* (Colorado Springs, CO: NavPress, 1995).
2. See "Evaluating Your Group" in Neal McBride, *How to Lead Small Groups* (Colorado Springs, CO: NavPress, 1990).

About the Author

Neal F. McBride (Ed.D, Indiana University; Ph.D., Oregon State University) is president of Grace University in Omaha, Nebraska. Dr. McBride's background includes serving as a seminary professor, professor of psychology, minister of education, youth pastor, church planter, and U.S. Air Force Reserve chaplain. He has worked with small groups of all kinds since 1969. Neal has written two other books published by NavPress, *How to Lead Small Groups* and *How to Build a Small Groups Ministry*.